IN PURSUIT

OF THE

GREAT WHITE RABBIT

REFLECTIONS ON A PRACTICAL SPIRITUALITY

EDWARD HAYS

Forest of Peace

Other Books by the Author:
(available from the publisher)

Prayers and Rituals
Psalms for Zero Gravity
Prayers for a Planetary Pilgrim
Prayers for the Domestic Church
Prayers for the Servants of God

Contemporary Spirituality
Holy Fools & Mad Hatters
The Old Hermit's Almanac
A Pilgrim's Almanac
Pray All Ways
The Lenten Labyrinth
A Lenten Hobo Honeymoon
Secular Sanctity
The Ascent of the Mountain of God
Feathers on the Wind

Parables and Stories
The Ladder
The Gospel of Gabriel
St. George and the Dragon
The Magic Lantern
The Ethiopian Tattoo Shop
Twelve and One-Half Keys
Sundancer
The Christmas Eve Storyteller
The Quest for the Flaming Pearl

IN PURSUIT OF THE GREAT WHITE RABBIT

copyright © 1990, by Edward M. Hays

Library of Congress Catalog Card Number: 90-84041
ISBN: 0-939516-13-6

published by
Forest of Peace
P.O. Box 428
Notre Dame, IN 46556
1-800-282-1865
www.avemariapress.com

printed by
Hall Commercial Printing
Topeka, KS 66608-007

1st printing: October 1990
2nd printing: February 1991
3rd printing: January 1992
4th printing: October 1994
5th printing: July 1999

6th Printing: February 2004

cover art and illustrations by
Edward Hays

IN PURSUIT

OF
THE

GREAT WHITE
RABBIT

PLAYFULLY DEDICATED

to my older and only sister
Jane
and to her 500 and some sisters,
the Sisters of Charity of Leavenworth

TABLE OF CONTENTS

PREFACE TO THE PURSUIT

Before you begin this book, I would like to take a few minutes to visit with you. The chapters in this book that you are about to read deal with ways and places in which you can experience God. Not very long ago it was commonly believed that only a rare handful of people could directly experience God. These fortunate few were called by the exotic name "mystics." The usual response to thinking of oneself as a mystic is much like being called "creative": we consider it valid only for a privileged few.

Yet everyone is naturally creative. The real issue is how each one of us can be more creative and can assist our creativity in finding expression. The same is true for being a mystic, for touching the Divine Mystery. Each of us has been divinely designed to be creative and mystical. The various chapters of this book are like the maps of treasure hunters. Their purpose is to help you explore your daily life for ways to see, taste, feel and touch the hidden treasure of God.

No one can remain passionately faithful to the spiritual quest on a diet of second-hand religious experiences. Simply reading about the lives of saints and mystics will not sustain a truly dynamic spiritual life. You yourself must go in pursuit of personal encounters with God. Richard McBrien has said that spirituality is a way of life based on an experience of God and shaped by that experience. Can anyone, then, have a valid spirituality without truly experiencing God? However, you need not travel to Tibet or to some special shrine in search of the Divine Mystery. An authentic spirituality, as Dr. John Pilch has shown, can flow from an experience of God within the value system of the mainstream culture of your native country.

May this small book assist you in finding the Great White Rabbit who is hidden in the midst of your home, family, friendships and work—and who can pop up at any time in your daily life.

Peace,

The Invisible White Rabbit

Does the name Elwood P. Dowd mean anything to you? Was he a former winner of the Nobel Prize or famous for discovering a virus vaccine? No, Elwood Dowd was a fictional character of the Broadway theater. He was perhaps one of the most lovable, happiest and most emotionally balanced characters ever created for the stage. Mary Chase won the Pulitzer Prize for the play in which Elwood was one of the central characters. He shared center stage with another personage from whom the play receives its name: Harvey!

Ah, I can see a smile crossing the face of many a reader! However, if you are unfamiliar with the play, Harvey was the best friend, confidant and drinking buddy of Elwood Dowd...and Harvey was a six-foot, invisible white rabbit! Mary Chase's marvelous story toys with the idea that someone who is so obviously insane that he has a six-foot rabbit as a constant companion can be so normal (or extraordinarily abnormal) that he is always kind and pleasant to everyone he meets.

Elwood and his friend Harvey become Broadway *parable* characters in the process of looking at some primary questions for those on a spiritual quest. Why do some people live their whole lives in a dynamic religious search while others never begin? Why do some begin with enthusiasm but abandon the quest after a period of time? Why do some continue their prayer and meditation but reach a point where they stop growing, overcome by the burdens of daily life? These are universal spiritual quandaries, reflected on by people of all creeds over the ages. One answer to these questions comes from this story from the early Christian hermits in the deserts of Egypt:

It seems that a young aspirant to holiness once came to visit the hermitage of an old holy man who was sitting in the doorway of his quarters at sunset. The old man's dog stretched out across the threshold as the young spiritual seeker presented his problem to the holy man. "Why is it, Abba, that some who seek God come to the desert and are zealous in prayer but leave after a year or so, while others, like you, remain faithful to the quest for a lifetime?"

The old man smiled and replied, "Let me tell you a story:

"One day I was sitting here quietly in the sun with my dog. Suddenly a large white rabbit ran across in front of us. Well, my dog jumped up, barking loudly, and took off after that big rabbit. He chased the rabbit over the hills with a passion. Soon, other dogs joined him, attracted by his barking. What a sight it was, as the pack of dogs ran barking across the creeks, up stony embankments and through thickets and thorns! Gradually, however, one by one, the other dogs dropped out of the pursuit, discouraged by the course and frustrated by the chase. Only my dog continued to hotly pursue the white rabbit.

"In that story, young man, is the answer to your question."

The young man sat in confused silence. Finally, he said, "Abba, I don't understand. What is the connection between the rabbit chase and the quest for holiness?"

"You fail to understand," answered the old hermit, "because you failed to ask the obvious question. Why didn't the other dogs continue on the chase? And the answer to that question is that they had not **seen** the rabbit. Unless you see your prey, the chase is just too difficult. You will lack the passion and determination necessary to perform all the hard work required by the discipline of your spiritual exercises.''

This opening reflection is about a primal prerequisite for the spiritual journey: **you must see the Rabbit!** If we don't have ⟵ a real experience of the Divine Mystery in some form, we will lack the energy necessary to keep up the pursuit for holiness. Like the dogs in the hermit's story, we will drop out of the race if we only follow the saints and mystics who have seen the Rabbit. If we are only caught up in the enthusiasm of others, we will fail to be constant in our search. **Each of us** must see the Rabbit!

Are we to wait then, like the hermit's dog, for the rabbit to appear in our lives? Was his resting on the hermitage doorstep a symbol for the prayer of waiting, for meditation? Or is the appearance of the rabbit more like what happened in *Harvey*? The following is from Mary Chase's play:

> **Elwood**: I had just helped Ed Hickey into a taxi. Ed had been mixing his rye with his gin, and I felt he needed conveying. I started to walk down the street when I heard a voice saying: "Good evening, Mr. Dowd." I turned, and there was this great white rabbit leaning against a lamp-post. Well, I thought nothing of that, because when you have lived in a town as long as I have lived in this one, you get used to the fact that everyone knows your name. Naturally, I went over to chat with him..."You have the advantage of me. You know my name and I don't know yours." Right back at me he said: "What name do you like?" Well, I didn't even have to think a minute: Harvey has always been a favorite name. So I said, "Harvey," and this is the interesting part of the whole thing. He said, "What a coincidence! My name happens to be Harvey."

The fact that Elwood quite readily accepted the unusual seemed

Openness to make him a prime candidate for the appearance of a six-foot white rabbit who called him by name. Such childlike openness seems also to be the first requirement for "Rabbit-seeing."

If we are to experience God, we must be open to God, to the mystical, to the divine, appearing in our lives. And we must have an openness that is free of any preconditions about **how** that will happen. Looking for God in a godly form is the great historical mistake. Do you look to find God in a burning bush (as Moses found God) or in any and all bushes—like the bush behind your garage? "Look for God in the spirea bush behind my garage?" you might ask in bewilderment. Exactly! Perhaps you remember the childhood puzzles which had pictures of a house and garden or a landscape. You were asked to find as many figures hidden in the picture as possible. There were animals and people in the trees and billowing clouds, and some were even hidden in the shapes of the stones in the chimney or the water of the brook. Searching in the ordinary things of life is one way you can begin to see the "Rabbit." The paradox is that ordinary and extraordinary are really the same—it all depends on how we look at what we see!

If all creation is a continuous outpouring of God, then all of life is the Rabbit. True mystics are not necessarily those who have visions, but rather those who have vision. They see the extraordinary, the mystical, in everyday events. If we desire such vision, we will have to give our brains a bath! Our minds must be cleansed of prejudgments about what God looks like. We will have to take a brush and scrub away all those grade school pictures of God and erase all the statements made by saints about their experience of the Divine Mystery. Only then can we begin to see the true picture.

But giving the brain a bath is much like giving a bath to a dog: the mind will jump and squirm and resist. As your mind struggles and soapsuds splash in your eyes, remember that without such a scrubbing you will not likely survive the difficult work of the spirit quest. A true vision of the Divine Mystery provides a nuclear core of energy for those who persevere in their search. The spiritual journey can test one to the limit. It requires constant self-discipline and watchfulness just to be ready to see the Rabbit. Then once the Rabbit appears, it requires constantly extending the boundaries of one's heart and mind. It means pushing back the known frontiers, climbing over the fences of our fears and moving outward and onward. It always remains a discipline, but it becomes easier as we proceed. We form more and more graceful patterns of behavior each time we retrace an act of kindness or compassion. In time the act of loving unselfishly becomes easier, but it will always remain a challenge. In short, the way is always uphill, for growing spiritually is an act of growing up. Holiness—and wholeness—involves an evolutionary ascent of our consciousness toward **more**! More love, more patience, more compassion, more prayerfulness. More is always expected if we want to grow as we are designed to grow—like God!

Because it is hard work, people of the Way often camp out. Sometimes we are tempted to camp, not overnight, but permanently! This sense of "stability" can tempt us to call ourselves "People of the Way." But, of course, when we set our tent stakes in concrete, we aren't going anywhere. Because spiritual growth always requires effort and we easily grow tired, we feel inclined to stop our growth at certain stages. However, just as a campsite is beginning to feel homey, the "inevitable" call seems to come: "Fold up your tent and move on...climb higher!" That call from God comes in countless ways, and we can find countless ways to check it, to close our hearts and ears so that we don't have to move on. However, we can be grateful that God, like a lover who won't take "no" for an answer, continues to visit us in a multitude of ways. While we should train our eyes to see the Divine Presence in such common things as a spirea bush or our next-door neighbor, let us not restrict God! We can hold ourselves open to the possibility that God can enter our lives in a manner that is outside the normal boundaries of what we call reality. God can come in a mystical religious experience.

The play *Harvey* suggests that a person can be happy by having an intimate friend and constant companion who is invisible. Elwood's friendship was at the heart of his joy. Our friendship with God can be a similar experience and equally central in our lives. Such mystical experiences, as well as the call to "fold up your tent and move on," are truly gifts. We prepare for them first by removing the barriers of intellect which say that such gifts are impossible. That is made easier by a realization that the twentieth and twenty-first centuries are not essentially different from the twelfth, ninth or first centuries. If there were mystics and mystical experiences in those ages, why not today? Moving beyond the prejudice of exclusively rational thinking and of our own doubts, we open ourselves to the possibility of the rare gift of experiencing God directly. Such an openness is central, even primal, to the spiritual pilgrimage. As the old hermit said, "Unless you see the Rabbit, the pursuit is just too difficult."

By remaining faithful to our dreams and our spirit quests, we may find ourselves, like Elwood P. Dowd, counted among the strange or eccentric. However, like Elwood, we may also find ourselves counted among the happiest and most-loved people on earth. As we struggle to expand the boundaries of our hearts and minds, embracing the hard work of the quest, we should "take heart" because daily we are coming closer and closer to the likeness of God. It is the same for anyone committed to a difficult task—whether a runner, artist, musician or pray-er. Each day the work, while remaining work, becomes easier and more joyful.

Tiny Alice

Do you remember the beginning of Lewis Carroll's charming book, *Alice in Wonderland?* Upon seeing a large white rabbit, Alice followed it down its hole. There she found herself in a room with many doors. A tiny golden key lay on a crystal table, but it was too small for all the locks. Then she saw a door only fifteen inches tall which the golden key fit perfectly. She opened the door, and on the other side was a beautiful garden with bright flowers and cool fountains. But, alas, poor Alice was far too large to pass through the small door that led to a narrow passage. Looking around, Alice saw on the same crystal table a small bottle with a label that read, ''Drink me.'' Alice did. At once she shrank to a height of only ten inches! She was thus able to continue her adventure.

Alice solved her big problem by using that little bottle. It was 1865 when Charles Dodgson, under the pen name Lewis Carroll, created the ''little bottle'' solution for Alice. Well over a century later, we too believe that the solution to one of our big problems may lie in the use of a little bottle. Only the instructions on this bottle read, ''Fill me!''

Fill it with what? With a sample of your urine, please! The ''big problem,'' of course, is drug abuse. The fact that over the past decade or so many Americans have seen drugs as an issue of greater importance than the economy, the national debt or the ever-escalating arms build-up has not been overlooked by politicians. Those seeking elected office have stampeded to join the crusade.

In 1986 President Reagan and the White House staff even offered to have their urine tested as a symbolic gesture to underscore the commitment of their program to create a "drug-free workplace for Americans." The use of drugs by youth as well as adults is truly a serious issue. Over twenty million Americans have taken cocaine, and millions more use other illegal drugs. We are all further aware that "legal" drugs, such as alcohol, are abused by so many others—three times the number of those on illegal drugs.

This chapter is about the drug abuse practiced by **each of us**. It is also about our common problem of being too large to slip through the tiny doorway. Our national leaders have advocated what we all desire: a drug-free workplace. The question that can so easily be lost from our consideration is, "From which drugs?" The use of drugs is not new to the world. Jesus and the other great spiritual masters addressed the issue. When asked by someone in the crowd, "Lord, are they few in number who are to be saved?" Jesus answered, "Try to come in through the narrow door. Many, I tell you, will try to enter and be unable" (Lk. 13: 23-24).

It seems that every one of us may have the same problem as poor Alice: we're all too big for the narrow door! "But," you might ask, "I don't see the connection between Jesus' warning about the narrow entrance to heaven and the issue of drug abuse."

In listening to the cries of alarm, one might believe that we are face to face with a terrible affliction that is new to this generation. In fact, America's drug problems are **not** new. In 1897, for example, more than one million pounds of raw opium were smuggled into the United States! Since the end of the Civil War, America has been involved in five different cycles of opium and cocaine abuse. The historical reality that American drug abuse tends to come and go doesn't mean that we shouldn't be concerned. We **do** need to ask if we are equally concerned about the drug problem that does not come and go in cycles but is continuously with us. It was **this** drug problem that was the primary concern of Jesus. And those who wish to enter through the narrow door of which he spoke will also have to be able to pass a test.

On the narrow door that leads to the Kingdom are inscribed the words: "You shall love God with all your heart, and your neighbor as yourself" (Mt. 22:29-31). There seems to be no problem with accepting, if not necessarily practicing, that commandment. All good Christians try to love God and others. Our prayers and songs are full of expressions of love. However, if we enter the doorway and glance over our shoulders at the back of the door, we will find another commandment: "You shall hate no one. You shall have **no** enemy, not even one!"

Suddenly the door frame shrinks until we have no chance of squeezing through. We **do** have enemies. We have national enemies, and we have personal enemies. There are people we do not like, those whom we avoid and those with whom we wage private little wars. We can't get through that narrow door because we have too many "ifs" in our pockets. Whose pockets aren't filled with "ifs"? For instance: "I will love you if you agree with me. I will love you if you are white, American, Christian, heterosexual and a Democrat." Now, don't misunderstand me; I know a lot of decent Republicans, but would you want your sister to marry one?

The world's oldest and most-used drug to "get high on" is bigotry. It always makes us "high," higher than others, no matter how low on the social scale we find ourselves. Someone has defined bigotry as "a personal dislike for someone whom you do not even know." Nearly as dangerous is a filtered form of this drug that is also very popular: snobbishness. Laced with disdain instead of raw hate, this drug is popular at tea parties and more refined social events.

Speaking to the crowds, Jesus said, "You have heard the commandment, 'You shall love your countrymen but hate your enemies.' My command to you is: love your enemies, pray for your persecutors. This will prove that you are children of God" (Mt. 5: 43). How unethical and mischievous of Jesus to misquote that ancient law of Leviticus! The law of Moses *did not* say that

- 17 -

one could hate one's enemy. Was Jesus being anti-Semitic or trying to upstage the teachings of Moses?

It seems that Jesus was mirroring back the popular interpretation of the law of Leviticus: "Love your fellow Jew but hate the Greek or Roman or Samaritan!" You and I, like the ancient Jews, also hold to our own interpretation of Jesus' law: "Love your brother/sister Christian but hate the Jew or the pagan Hindu or Buddhist. Love Americans but make war against the Communists." Yes, we have cultural, religious and national enemies. We also have personal enemies: people we dislike or just plain can't stand!

The urine of drug users contains traces of the drugs they have taken. If there were a urine test at the "narrow door" that leads to salvation, could any of us pass the test? That only a few people will "squeeze by" is a hard reality for believers in Jesus Christ to accept. We have our little gold key of Baptism, guaranteed to open the gates of heaven. But while we can open the door, is it not too narrow for us to enter?

When Christians come together to worship, especially to share in the breaking of the bread, to keep the memorial of the death and resurrection of Jesus, it may be necessary to add a new ritual. At the front door of the gathering place, you would be given a little brown bottle. Yes, that's right—a urine test! You would be asked to step into the rest room and fill the bottle. Then it would be tested. If no trace of the world's oldest and most universal drug were found, you could enter. Remember that in casual users no trace of the drug remains in the urine after four or five days. On the other hand, if on the night before you came to worship you had gotten even a little "high" on bigotry, snobbishness or raw hate, you would not be able to pass the test!

While this ritual proposal may be new, the concept isn't. Being "drug-free" was a major requirement in the early Church. The *Didache*, a document called "The Teaching of the Twelve Apostles," written around the year 120 A.D., makes this statement:

> On the Lord's Day, gather in community to break bread
> and offer thanks. But confess your sins first, so that your

sacrifice may be a pure one. No one who has a quarrel with a brother (sister) may join your gathering: not until all are reconciled. Your sacrifice must not be made unholy.

A drug found in the urine of each of us is the oldest and most deadly of all drugs: traces of anger, hate and war—from the president down to the smallest child—are present in our urine! Karl Marx said that religion is the opium of the people, but he was wrong. The drug that really "turns people on" is **hate**. If your urine were tested today, would it be free of this drug in its raw or refined forms? Our *enemies* may be the Communists, the Iranians, the pro-choicers or even Mrs. Disagreeable who lives down the street or Mr. Rude who works in our office. America's drug problem comes and goes in cycles, but our greatest drug problem has been with us since East of Eden, since Cain and Abel.

Jesus sought to remove the oldest problem of humanity, but he knew that evil cannot be outlawed—war and hate do not obey laws. At best, civil or religious laws only limit hate. Jesus gave us a positive command containing its reverse negative: "You shall love...You shall not hate." However, can you and I pass the *Didache* test? Have you, for the past four or five days, abstained from negative thoughts or unloving behavior not only toward your family or neighbors, but toward the clerk behind the counter or the cop on the corner? Remember, it takes four or five days to filter out the traces of even casual contempt for another. If we are honest, we realize that we stand before the narrow door as Alice did, knowing that we can't squeeze through.

The Gospel, however, is "good news." So what's the good news for us who got "F's" on our urine-drug-doorway test? The good news is found right in our urine, at least in the process that makes it. The human body is wondrously designed; urine is the river that carries away the impurities in our blood. Our blood flows through cleansing glands called kidneys, passing through a million tiny coiled tubes which filter out the poisonous elements. In this process kidneys produce an amber-colored liquid called urine—about one and one-half quarts a day. As we dispose of urine, we also remove from our bodies those deadly impurities.

We do not usually consciously consume impurities; they are

by-products of the food we eat and the workings of our bodies. However, if these poisons are not flushed out, the result is inevitably painful sickness and then death! The process of hate is much the same. We do not usually consciously think unkind thoughts; they just pop into our heads. Generally they are the by-products of living with other people.

Part of being human involves being attracted to some people and being "turned off" by others, loving some and disliking others. In the normal course of our day, we are likely to have a number of disagreements with others. This is natural. However, if the negative thoughts and feelings that surround these differences are not removed from our hearts, we soon become poisoned.

Some time ago, American television carried an interview with an aged political leader from India. During the course of the interview, the Indian spoke of his daily ritual of drinking his own urine! He attributed his good health and vitality to this ancient health practice. The American viewing audience was horrified. Yet, whenever we allow negative and angry thoughts to constantly recycle in our minds, without opening them to prayer, we are involved in just such a practice—without its healing benefits.

In the Letter to the Ephesians is found the admonition that we are not to let the sun go down on our anger (Eph. 4: 26). Implied in this passage is the reality that there are days when we will be angry or involved in an emotionally costly private war with another. To address this condition of being human, Jesus told his disciples to "pray always!" Prayer is like the cleansing process of our kidneys because it flushes out the traces of life's most deadly drugs: anger, hate, bigotry, snobbishness and our perpetual tribal and personal addiction to war and violence. Don't fear those drugs that can kill the body, but rather those that can destroy your soul!

So if you want to be able to pass through the small and very narrow door leading to the Kingdom and to salvation, then pray always. Pray for those who hurt you, for those who get on your nerves, who irritate you and make you angry. You can make their names like a mantra that you repeat over and over, holding them firmly in your heart, placing them on Christ's altar, in that place of love. Prayer purifies the inner person and cleanses the heart, just as the kidneys continuously cleanse the blood of its deadly impurities.

Perhaps a new personal and very private ritual might remind us of this very necessary purification process. This new prayer ritual could make saints out of beer drinkers! Each time you are involved in that wondrous and necessary process of passing urine, you could pray:

O God, grant to your servant
that as my body now flushes out its physical impurities,
all negative, harmful and angry feelings within me
may be flushed out as well.

Amen.

Private Little "Holy Wars"

Many of us are familiar today with the Arabic term *Jehad* which means "Holy War." Various Islamic countries of the Near East speak of waging "holy wars." To some Moslems, a *Jehad* is a call to the whole Islamic world to take arms against the "unbelievers." We also know that "holy wars" are not the sole property of Moslems. The history of Christianity is blotted with them. The Crusades were carried on for centuries. The Thirty Years' War and the twelfth century war waged in southern France against the Albigenses (a small religious sect) were also called "holy wars."

While the term "holy war" may seem totally contradictory to "enlightened" people, most of us still do battle in the name of God. A holy war is one where hostilities are entered into for "just" reasons, especially when the motivation is religious. However, not all holy wars are waged between groups of religious zealots, nor are all of them "declared" wars. It would be good to reflect on the "holy" wars in which each of us tend to engage. Such wars help create a "fertile" climate for conflict, aggression and the destruction of property and people's lives across our tiny planet.

However, let us begin this reflection with a proposed movie plot. Inspired by intergalactic combat movies such as *Star Wars*, it may help us appreciate how our private little wars can have global consequences.

The opening scene of the movie shows a space probe, conducted by a race of people from some far-away galaxy. Its mission is to bring back information about a distant star which these people call the "Morning Star." This brilliant star has long been a source of poetic inspiration and religious symbolism for them. The intergalactic space probe comes within 10,000 light years of this fascinating star and begins to photograph it for scientific research. The first photographs taken by their long-range lenses (advanced far beyond our present cameras) surprisingly reveal that the object is not a star but rather a beautiful blue and green planet. Then, with the use of laser X-ray cameras, the crew of the space probe discovers that it is far different from the usual gaseous or volcanic planet. The X-ray photos show that beneath the calm external appearance of solid material form, it is in reality an enormous luminous web! This web-work planet is composed of billions upon billions of connected fibers which crisscross one another in a maze of intersections. Unlike most webs, which are only two dimensional, this is a three dimensional, spheric web from which is emitted a brilliant bluish diamond light. The space probe returns to its home planet base to make its report. It reveals to the anxiously awaiting people that the mystery of the Morning Star is that it is not a star and not even just a planet but a living organism traveling in space. They suggest that it is ALIVE, luminously beautiful and perhaps—perhaps—it is also conscious!

THE END

As you may have guessed by now, this movie is not about the Morning Star but the living, webbed organism called Earth!

The present photographs of our small planet have been taken only from what amounts to our front yard. We have traveled just a short distance into space, and our still-primitive photographic equipment allows us to show only the externals of our tiny space ship named Earth. The proposed movie plot that began this reflection could be viewed as just another space fantasy—except that sorcerers, medicine men and women, shamans and mystics of all ages have spoken about Earth as a web of life. Like the Native American Indians, they knew without laser photography that Earth is not a solid object. Rather all life is woven together in a web. This "web" is a field of energy interlaced with invisible fibers. Plants, animals, humans—all that exists is interconnected. What happens to even the least part of the web has an unalterable effect upon the whole.

Contrary to "common sense" or surface observation, the scientific conclusions of quantum physics tell us that our earth is not composed of blocks of matter. Essentially, all the physical universe is made up of energy. If we are to understand who we are and something about the world we live in, we need to take a closer look at energy.

Energy vibrates at different frequencies, from very slow to extremely rapid. The frequency of the vibration affects what form any given energy takes. Further, there is a law of quantum physics that reads, "Energy of a certain essence, speed or vibration tends to attract other energy of a similar vibration or speed."

Your thoughts, which you may regard as without physical effect because they do not have mass or weight, are forms of energy that have a great deal of effect! If your thoughts are of deep intensity, they create their own magnetic field which, as we saw, attracts energy of a similar pattern or vibration. Thoughts operate according to that old adage: "Like attracts like." Every thought we have is like a magical blueprint which holds the power to act as a magnet. It draws whatever forms, shapes, ideas, energy and even people that will make the thought-blueprint a reality! This was well understood by mystics and spiritual masters, particularly by Jesus and Buddha. In the opening passage of the *Dhammapada*, the words of the Lord Buddha, we read, "With our thoughts we make our world. Think evil thoughts and evil will follow you as surely as the cart follows the ox." But before we explore the words of Jesus about our thoughts, let us explore the magic of magnets.

Many of us recall playing with horseshoe-shaped magnets as children, using them to pick up nails and other bits of metal. There are magnets, much more powerful and often hidden from our view, that perform daily magic in our lives. Today, magnets make possible the electric power needed to operate the typewriter I'm using to write to you. In telephones and radios, magnets allow us to hear sounds over great distances.

Magnets got their name from the legend that says they were discovered long ago in Asia Minor in a place called Magnesia. Stones in that part of what is present-day Turkey held "magical" powers which drew them to iron. When these stones were suspended from a string, a wondrous thing happened—they swung toward the North Star!

These stones, called "leadstones" or "lodestones," made possible the voyages of Columbus and other explorers, for the magnet was the mother of the compass. Compasses allowed travelers to journey during the daylight, when the stars were not visible. No one knew exactly how they worked until 1600 when an English scientist discovered an astonishing fact. The entire planet is one large magnet which causes the north pole to pull the needle of a compass toward it.

Part of the marvel of the magnet is that any object drawn to it also becomes magnetic, gaining the same power to attract. As children we saw this fact proved when we picked up a bunch of nails with a magnet. Nails that were held by the force field of the magnet had the power to hold other nails. This power of a single nail to attract others remains only as long as it stays in contact with the magnet. Now, we can understand better the words of Jesus, which at first hearing sound strangely strict: "You have heard the commandment imposed on your foreparents, 'You shall not commit murder: every murderer will be liable to judgment.' What I say to you is that those who grow angry with a sister or brother will be liable to judgment...and if they hold another in contempt, they risk the fires of Gehenna" (Mt. 5: 21-23).

Jesus seems to say, "Beware, little ones! When you think evil, you only draw evil to yourselves, even though the evil and angry thoughts are directed toward others. You call harm down upon

your enemies and yourselves." The magnetic law of energy applies just as well to the force field of the mind as it does to the force field we call Earth. When we think hostile and angry thoughts, we draw evil to evil and violence to violence as surely as the nail is drawn to the magnet. Our thoughts are also energy forms which we project outward along the fibers of the web, affecting all creation, since it is all one great magnetic field of energy.

I have serious doubts about whether there is really such a thing as a holy war. All wars, between nations or among those who live in the same house, affect the entire web of the universe. When we nurture resentment, dislike or hate for another person—even when we feel that ours is a just and "holy" cause—we set into motion vibrations of destruction. When we think that how we feel about another person is only between the two of us, we simply are not sensitive to the intricate webwork of which we are a part. Such a lack of awareness helps fertilize the world for devastation. This, of course, is not to say that we should deny our feelings. Indeed, we need to accept and even embrace our feelings and thoughts. But the more we are aware of our interrelatedness with all of life, the more our ways of thinking and feeling change—and the more the whole world can change. The survival of our planet may well be served by crying out in protest against the arms build-up. Such a protest, however, is only an exercise in pride if we have not first disarmed our minds of every negative, judgmental and harmful thought! It is when we disarm the missiles of our minds that we really do something about war and the massive build-up of nuclear missiles.

Anger and distrust are powerful weapons. At the same time, we can rejoice that, while angry thoughts breed evil, peaceful thoughts are equally powerful tools for bringing about the Kingdom over all the earth. When we seek the way of holiness with an intensity, a passion, that which is holy will be drawn to us. "Seek first," said Jesus, "God's kingship over you, God's way of holiness, and all will be given you besides" (Mt. 6: 32). By setting our minds on the way of God, we draw the divine to ourselves—and with it the love and courage we need for daily life. And the more conscious of the divine we become, the more we become aware of our participation in the divine webwork.

When we allow our mind to be homes for thoughts of peace, harmony and love, we also begin to radiate those qualities magnetically outward along the web of creation. In chapter four of the *Dhammapada* Buddha says, "The perfume of sandalwood or jasmine cannot travel against the wind. But the fragrance of virtue travels even against the wind, as far as the ends of the world." How else does virtue travel to the ends of the earth but along the fibers, the invisible nerve linkages, which connect all that is. Love and virtue issue forth to the very edges of the earth— and perhaps to the farthest corners of the cosmos! As we cultivate this holy climate, we bring peace and good things to ourselves as well. The wisdom of Jesus and Buddha is also expressed by the Chinese sage Lao Tsu. In the twenty-second chapter of the *Tao Te Ching* we read, "Be really whole and all things will come to you." **All** things—not simply food, clothing and drink—will come to you. That is a large promise, yet it is echoed by King David in the Psalms of Israel: "If you find your delight in God, God will grant your heart's desire" (Ps. 36: 4). Make God the delight of your heart, and along the vast network of earth's interconnecting fibers, you will attract everything you need, all your heart's desires.

The messages of Jesus, Buddha, Lao Tsu and King David are all on similar frequencies of the divine web-field. Be sensitive, then, to the gentle tugs of the web as you ponder another mystery: where is the center of this vast webwork? In a real way, it is right at the center of your own heart! What you think and seek with passion directly affects the entire web. And when you pray, when you sit in the stillness of meditation, reflect on the words of the seventeenth century English poet, John Dryden:

> Our souls sit close and silently within
> And their own webs from their own sense is such
> That spider-like, we feel the tenderest touch.

As we sit close, when we sit silently within, united with others—even if they are far away—we can feel the tenderest touch upon the web. When we put aside our "anxious cares about what we shall wear, what we shall eat or drink" (Mt. 6: 25), we open ourselves to the marvelous movements of the entire web.

Jesus and the other spiritual masters knew that the web exists. We have all experienced tender tugs upon the web. Who has not sometimes felt the presence of another in a thought just before the telephone rang or a letter arrived. When we are conscious that such a pattern is a reality, we open ourselves more fully to the power of its force field. When we keep attempting to stay in touch with the web and to bring it into clearer focus, we further know its power. This consciousness helps us to go to our prayer with great respect, seeing it not as a "pious practice" but as an activity of enormous importance. By the same token, it also increases our respect for the lethal power of all negative, harmful and angry thoughts directed toward others. When the mystery of how all creation intertwines is understood, only a fool would dare to court destruction by thinking violent thoughts.

Those of us who live in the industrial world are likely to have only a marginal contact with the mystery of the web. Our daily lives are surrounded with concrete, steel and asphalt. We eat artificially colored food and drink chemically treated beverages from paper and plastic containers. In order to become more sensitive to the web and its interwoven connections, we would do well to return to a more direct contact with the earth and with earthy things. Pre-industrial peoples naturally understood that all of life is one living organism because they lived in immediate contact with nature. When we reach out to touch, in various ways, the thick outer shell of the web, we begin to realize that at its heart is the Heart of all life, the Source of all creation.

Confronted with the immense threat of nuclear escalation and the seemingly permanent presence of war, we ordinary people are tempted to ask, "But what can I do?" The answer is as simple as it is challenging. We can make our homes and our lives an environment that is real instead of artificial, an environment in touch with the stirrings of the web. We can sit still in silence and meditation, in quiet prayer, to become more sensitive and responsive. And first and foremost, we can recognize the king/queenship of God and the divine way of holiness and wholeness. Only then will all war, "holy" or otherwise, become as offensive as human slavery and as evil as sin. Only then will war begin to fade from the web we call Earth.

The Seeds of Change

The seeds of change are all around us at the dawning of a new century. Yet the call to change is as old as Moses and is at the heart of the Gospels. In fact, the overture of the "Good News" has John the Baptist echoing the words of Isaiah, "Make straight the way of the Lord." Although it's not even Christmas time, a melody from my childhood came to me the other day, a tune that harmonizes with the message of John:

> Oh, you'd better watch out, you'd better not cry,
> you'd better not pout, I'm tellin' you why:
> Santa Claus is comin' to town.
> He knows when you are sleeping; he knows when
>   you're awake.
> He knows when you've been bad or good.
> So be good for goodness'sake.

The message of that song could be summed up, "Straighten up, or Santa won't slide down **your** chimney!" Making straight the way of the Lord and "straightening up" are in reality the same work. As a child I often heard the words, "Edward, straighten up!" when my behavior was temporarily crooked. It usually happened when I didn't get what I wanted, when I wanted it.

Like all children my response to disappointment was to cry.

Ah, the tearful cries I hear today in toy departments (which I enjoy visiting) remind me of how I once responded to frustration. And having been told not to cry, I would often slip into the classic second-gear response and begin to pout. Would that these were the coping tools of little children only! How easily we fall into them as adults, though they may be done in a more sophisticated style. Strange, isn't it, how little we change with the passage of years? However, while our behavior patterns tend to remain the same, the song of John in the Jordan and the one about Santa coming to town both call us to straighten the crooked ways of our lives. Such a radical change is not easy, as this adaptation of an old Russian fairy tale shows:

> Once upon a time there was a merchant named Nikita the Mean (mean in the sense of miserly). One day while walking through Nikita's village, a beggar approached the old miser, pleading, "For Christ's sweet sake, kind merchant, please give me a pittance, for I am hungry." But Nikita the Mean walked on as if he were stone-deaf. Now a poor peasant walking behind Nikita took pity on the beggar and gave him a kopeck (it takes one hundred kopecks to make a single ruble). Nikita looked around and saw everyone watching and felt ashamed. So he said to the poor peasant, "Listen, little brother, lend me a kopeck. I want to give something to this poor beggar, but I don't have any small change."
>
> So the peasant gave him a coin, asking, "When, sir, shall I come to collect my loan?"
>
> As he hurried off, Nikita the Mean answered, "Come tomorrow, little brother."
>
> The next day the peasant came to the house of the merchant and asked, "Is Nikita the Mean at home?"
>
> Now he was, but he hid under his bed, instructing his wife to tell the peasant that he was away on business. The following day, the peasant caught Nikita at the front gates of his grand home and asked for his kopeck. "Sorry, my dear friend," replied Nikita, "but I don't have any change on me at this moment. Can you return later?"

"I shall come back next week," answered the peasant.

A week later when Nikita saw the peasant coming up the road, he said to his wife, "Listen, woman, I will quickly undress and lie naked at the foot of the ikons, and you will cover me with the burial shroud. When that peasant comes in, you will weep and lament as if I were dead. When he asks about his loan to me, tell him that I have just dropped dead."

When the peasant heard the news, wrapped in the tears of Nikita's wife, he said, "What a shame! He was such a kind and generous man, especially to the poor. Allow me the honor of washing his body."

Before the woman could object, the peasant snatched a kettle of boiling water from the stove and poured it all over Nikita's body. Now Nikita the Mean could hardly stand the pain, but he gritted his teeth and only one foot twitched, which the peasant pretended not to see. Putting the empty kettle back on the stove, the peasant said, "I will get his coffin, and we will carry kind Nikita to the church. But go and get all his gold, for it is only right that we bury it with him. He loved it so much." Nikita's wife, unable to object, helped the peasant fill the coffin with gold and jewels. Last of all they laid Nikita's golden saber on his chest with reverence and closed the coffin.

At the church they placed his coffin before the altar, and, as Nikita's wife wept, the peasant prayed the psalms of burial. About midnight they heard a window being opened and saw thieves preparing to enter the village church. Quickly the peasant and Nikita's wife hid themselves behind the altar. The thieves were carrying their evening's loot of gold and silver coins which they dumped on Nikita's coffin, using it as a counting table. Having divided their spoils from a very successful night's looting, they opened the coffin and exclaimed with wonder, "Look at this, a king's treasure!" They then began to empty the coffin of all its gold. Poor Nikita was so frightened that he couldn't move a muscle, even though his beloved gold was now in the hands of robbers. He thought to himself, "These thieves may be apprehended by the police, and I will get my money back. But if that peasant knows that I am alive, he will take back his kopeck, and I will never see it again."

Soon the robbers began to fight amongst themselves about who should get Nikita's golden saber. As they shouted at one another, the peasant jumped out from his hiding place and said, "Whoever cuts off the dead man's head shall have his saber!"

Hearing this, Nikita the Mean, beside himself with fear, jumped out of his coffin. At the sight of the dead man bounding from his casket, the thieves ran from the church, leaving all their loot behind. When they were out of sight, Nikita's heart stopped pounding. He turned and said to the peasant, "Now, little brother, let us share all this loot of the robbers. Since I worked so much harder for it, I will take the larger share." Even with the uneven division, the peasant received a large sum of gold, more than enough to make him wealthy for life.

As they were leaving the church, the peasant turned and asked, "Friend, how about the kopeck you owe me?"

And Nikita, both arms loaded with gold, said, "Ah, good and dear brother, as you can see for yourself, I do not have any small change!" And Nikita the Mean never did pay back that kopeck.

This story suggests how tightly we tend to hold to our old bad habits. The passing of time only seems to strengthen them. You and I, like Nikita the Mean, can pass through life—we can be challenged by experiences that come close to death itself—and still not change. If we are honest about it, the number of reformed Scrooges is few compared to the vast majority of unchanged Nikitas. An old rabbi was once asked why the Messiah had not come. He responded, "The Messiah, blessed be his name, does not come because we are no different than we were yesterday."

The wise ones of the Torah speak of the emotions as being children of our thoughts. Understanding this is central in our desire to change our moods, our emotional responses, which have the power to push us around and cause us to be crooked in life. Change comes in life when we are able to make a distinction between what we feel like doing and what clearly needs to be done, no matter how unappealing it may seem. If we always wait until we are "in the mood" to pray, then prayer will never be a liberating factor in our lives. Prayer, especially meditational prayer, can happen very gracefully and spontaneously. However, it is also a discipline that requires practice regardless of how we may feel at a given moment. In the prayer of meditation we become aware that within our own person is a variety of feelings and thoughts. Meditation, with its discipline of gently returning to one's center, reveals that there is an "I" that is more essential to who we really are than the fleeting emotions and thoughts with which we tend to identify ourselves. That "I" passionately seeks the liberating changes needed for happiness and holiness.

Emotions not only shape behavior but can flow from it. We can experience higher and richer emotion by performing acts which our higher selves call us to do. For example, when we are not in the mood to serve the needs of others but do so anyway, moving from self-concern to a compassion for others, we can experience the emotion of joy in serving. In that joy we find new energy. This does not mean that we need to deny our lack of zeal because of being tired. We are not called to deny our humanity but to fulfill it. When we embrace how we feel as part of who we are at the moment, we can acknowledge, "I am tired and do not care to serve, but I also want to be of service . . . ." This sort of gentle self-discipline wedded to an honest self-acceptance and compassion for the self who sometimes has contrary desires, is the beginning of true compassion for others. Such honest compassion enables us to go beyond ourselves.

Permanent change comes when we begin at the beginning. Emotions, if you recall, are children of our thoughts. So we first need to plant a carefully chosen thought. Daily we need to support and nurture that thought with love. The thought grows into an act which, when repeated day after day, grows into a habit. A well-nurtured habit quickly grows into a personality, and before you know it . . . . This process rests on the assumption that you and I know why we should change. And why should we change?

This question brings us back to the song about Santa coming to town: "He knows when you've been bad or good. So be good for goodness' sake." What a marvelous last line: "So be good **for goodness' sake**." Be good not for the sake of a reward or to escape punishment, but be good for GOoDness' sake. Change whatever needs changing within you for the sake of the GOoD, the Holy, and not to influence people or win friends, not to get what you want—even happiness. Change for the sake of GOoDness alone.

Here is one more story to close this reflection:

> According to Islamic mystics, there was once a religious, church-going man who believed that it was his duty to help others stop sinning. He felt it was his duty to call them to reform their lives and change their sinful behavior. This religious man lived next door to a man who gambled excessively. The gambling man frequently prayed to be freed of his addiction and spoke to friends of this desire. However, like a lot of us, he continued in his bad habit.
>
> Each time he left home to go gambling and drinking, his pious neighbor would place a stone in his yard to mark his neighbor's sin. Each time the weak neighbor left to go to the gambling house he felt guilty, and each time he returned home he saw another stone on the pile. With each stone he placed upon the pile, the pious neighbor felt more anger toward his unconverted neighbor. He also felt a personal pleasure, which he called godliness, in having recorded another sin.
>
> This pattern went on for over twenty years. Each time the gambler saw his pious neighbor he would say, "Would that I understood goodness! Look at how concerned my neighbor is for my soul. How I wish I could change my ways and become like him, because I know that one day soon I must face my God."
>
> Now it so happened that one night a great storm fell upon the town. The violence of the storm was so im-

mediate and so great that both neighbors died within the same hour. An angel came to the gambler and said, "Come with me. You are to enter paradise this very hour!"

The gambler looked shocked and exclaimed, "There must be a mistake! You see, I am a sinner who is unconverted even though my good neighbor has tried for over twenty years to call me to goodness. You have made a mistake. The man you are to take to paradise lives next door."

"No," replied the angel, "your neighbor is being sent down to the lowest regions where he will be roasted over a great roaring fire."

"What kind of justice is that?" replied the gambler. "He attended worship faithfully each week; he worked without tiring for my conversion. I am sorry, but you must have your instructions reversed."

"There has been no error," said the angel, picking up the gambler and starting heavenward. "I will explain. Your pious neighbor has indulged himself for twenty years with feelings of superiority. He put all the stones on that great pile for **himself**, not for you."

"But," answered the gambler, "why am I being rewarded; what good in life have I done?"

"You," answered the angel, "are being rewarded because every time you saw your pious, but inwardly hostile, neighbor, you thought first of goodness, saying to yourself, 'Would that I understood goodness.' Then you thought about your neighbor's supposed virtue. It is goodness that is rewarding you. You are being rewarded not because of justice but for your fidelity in seeking goodness!"

When you hear those mystic words sung: "He knows when you've been bad or good. So be good for goodness' sake," recall this reflection on Nikita the Mean and the gambler—and plant a thought.

The Mother of Invention

There is a story about a man faced with such difficulty that he prayed on his knees for days on end that God would save him. In his prayer he vowed that if rescued from his distress, he would sell his home and give all the money from the sale to the poor. Now it came to pass that his prayer was heard and the grave problem was resolved. But now that the trouble had passed, the man had second thoughts about his vow. Since his home was worth a great deal of money, he devised a plan. He would place his home for sale but on the condition that the buyer must also purchase his cat. He had little difficulty selling his home and the cat that went with it. The home he sold for $100 and the cat for $199,900. The money from the house he gave to the poor, and the money from the sale of the cat he kept for himself!

Ah, the wisdom of the world, the ingenuity of the clever, which the ancient Latin writer expressed as *Mater Artium Necessitas*, "Necessity is the Mother of Invention." We who live at the breaking open of a new century have seen so many of the children of Mother Necessity. Our lives are awash in a flood of miracles and wonders that have sprung from the womb of necessity. Let's look at just a few of these.

Several years ago a small California company introduced an electronic marvel no larger than a paperback book. The instrument monitors forty-four key functions in an automobile. This "child" of Mother Necessity was designed to anticipate future problems in our cars and thus increase their life-expectancy and efficiency.

Confronted with the ominous and growing threat of cancer, a new body scanner, MNR, was recently invented. It has the capacity to detect cancer cells within days of their formation, as well as other minute physiological changes in our bodies. And all this without X rays!

Another company is in the process of producing low-cost photovoltaic panels that can be placed on one side of the roofs of our homes. These panels are intended to address the need to make houses energy self-sufficient at a low cost.

A tin can has been invented that is self-cooking. All you have to do is flip the tab-top and you will have hot food in minutes. A great way to address the need for a hot "brown bag" lunch!

An Atlantic fishery, faced with extinction at the hands of foreign competition, has produced a new plastic packaging that will keep fish fresh, without freezing, for two years!

New drugs of all types are constantly being created. One, for example, slows down "free radicals," the substances in our bodies that cause skin decay, aging, heart disease and certain forms of cancer. Also, a new band-aid has been designed that not only covers a wound but administers medicine through the skin.

The list of recent children of Mother Necessity could fill an entire volume. We rejoice that science, industry and medicine are facing the necessities of our age in such creative and inventive ways. How different are our lives because of all the progress and creativity of the past thirty years. As we look at inventions in these and other areas of life such as electronics and transportation, we also see that they are in a constant state of improvement and progress.

What do we see, though, when we look at the world of religion, spirituality and prayer? Are there any great leaps forward, any real creativity or inventiveness in regard to the moral or spiritual issues of the day? Perhaps the reason for a lack of inventiveness is the fact that we spend so little time or energy on our inward growth. Our focus on the external world is so consuming that we often feel we have no time or energy left for spiritual growth.

Perhaps another reason is that we see no necessity, no need to hurry when it comes to the spiritual. It's easy to say, "What's the urgent need? We have lots of time to change. I'll pray when I retire...when I finish this project...when I find a good spiritual director." The possible excuses and reasons for delay are endless! Beyond that, there are plenty of excuses for a lack of creativity or growth seemingly built into organized religions. If the religions of the world had a monopoly on transportation, who knows, we might all still be traveling by horse and buggy! One reason for religion's failure to respond to Mother Necessity is all the petty arguments that are raised to prevent communion and unity among different religious traditions. Another frequently heard excuse for any new, creative or inventive solution to a problem is, "Change takes time. We must respect our traditions."

The man in the parable at the beginning of this reflection showed the creative inventiveness that has been praised by the great spiritual leaders of history. Remember the words of Jesus about the clever, embezzling steward, "the worldly take more initiative than the other-worldly" (Lk. 16: 8). Necessity has a great deal to do with ingenuity. Maybe it is our failure to see the necessity for change, growth and creativity in our spiritual lives that accounts for why we accept as normal our shallow spiritual consciousness.

If we will allow her, Mother Necessity can lead us to the window of life and show us the world. She can also show us what time it is. This age in which we live is ending. A new order is already breaking through the framework of the old one. It will require of us a new consciousness, a new way of seeing and evaluating and a new way of simple living. Most of all it will require a new way of loving! There is, in reality, little time left. The new order will shake our personal foundations if we don't anticipate it. We must learn a new, fuller way to love, for the old ways, the ways we have grown up with, are insufficient for this dawning era. Thomas Parnell, the seventeenth century Irish poet, wrote,

Let those love who never loved before.
Let those who always loved now love the more.

Jesus said much the same thing. He called the world, almost two thousand years ago, to move beyond the traditional ways of loving. Jesus challenged the world to move beyond the love of one's spouse, children, aunts and uncles, a few dogs and a donkey or two to love in a much wider sense. He challenged us to move beyond family, beyond clan and even nation, to love on a truly global scale.

In those two thousand years we have seen some inspiring examples of such growth in loving and in consciousness. We rejoice—and even take pride—in people like Francis of Assisi, Theresa of Avila, Gandhi or Mother Theresa. But are they really a source of pride or embarrassment? Why have so few been able to raise their consciousness, to find a way of loving more fully and in a more evolved way? Why did it take the human family almost nineteen centuries to outgrow slavery? We still see its seeds in racial discrimination around the world. Then there is the issue of global disarmament. The very presence of nuclear arms reveals how we still think that war and weapons can be the ultimate solution to our problems.

Condemning nuclear weapons may be essential to our even living to see the new order. It is not, however, the entire solution. We must do something. We must begin to learn how to expand and mature in spirit in order to keep pace with our expanding technology. We must, in the words of Thomas Parnell, "love the more." Mother Necessity is shouting at us that our lives and the very life of the planet and the human race are at stake. We cannot just sit idly by. We must do something!

How can we learn to love in a different way? First, we should examine what we already know. As small children we learned an important social lesson. We learned that love is conditional. We learned that we must earn or deserve love. That love is not given freely—is not unconditional—is the lesson. Children find out quickly that if they want to be loved, they must behave in certain acceptable ways, reach certain levels of intellectual or physical achievement or conform to certain moral, social or religious patterns. If we are truly grown up, we must realize that such limited loving, such conditional love, is the pattern of the past. We must now learn to love others freely, to love them as they are, not as we want them to be. We must learn to love life as it is, not as we want it to be.

Unless we can come to love in this way, then war will continue to be the norm of the day, the business of life between nations, between wives and husbands, parents and children, between you and me! Attar of Nishapur, a great Islamic sage and saint, told the following story:

> Some Israelites reviled Jesus one day as he was walking through their village. But he answered by blessing them and praying for them. Someone said to Jesus, "You blessed these men, did you not feel anger towards them?" And he answered, "I could only spend of what I had in my purse."

Because war is still a condition of our hearts, we must change our hearts, our minds and the inadequate lessons about loving that we have embraced. The response of Jesus in the Islamic parable was possible because his heart was full of love— unconditional love. He blessed those who praised him and those who cursed him, because his heart was overflowing with blessings.

Mother Necessity cries out to us, "LOOK AT THE WORLD...LOOK AT WHAT TIME IT IS. CHANGE AND CHANGE NOW!" We cannot do nothing, just passively letting business go on as usual. We must all do something. Our awareness of the urgent necessity to live and love as did Jesus and the other holy ones of the past is calling forth one of the greatest religious movements in all history. It has already begun,

- 43 -

and it will bring about a quantum leap in spiritual consciousness for the human race.

Those who wish to be part of this cosmic spiritual movement must realize that it is built upon the "pebble theory." Throw a pebble into a pond and it will produce a tiny ring where it enters the water. Then slightly larger rings ripple outward from the first ring—wider and wider, larger and larger grow the rings. If we wish to do something in response to Mother Necessity, we can begin at the smallest ring or circle of our lives. Begin to love those around you with an unconditional love, accepting them as they are, with all their gifts and talents and their failings. Simply love them!

All truly great revolutions begin at one's fingertips. We join those tips together in prayer. They become empowered to respond to Mother Necessity during times of silent listening—centering prayer or meditation. In such times of silence we can begin to see what we must see. We begin to hear messages coming from the Divine Mystery, calling us to a quantum leap in the evolution of our human consciousness.

However, more than prayer is necessary. We must also abandon our passion for melodrama, our own little melodramas. When we direct our limited human energies to petty and trivial issues, we have little left for spiritual growth. When we magnify the normal ups and downs of daily living in a theatrical way to make our lives more interesting, we drain the spirit of its power to grow. You know the melodramas: "Why don't you put oil in the car, do you want to ruin the engine?…What do you mean, we don't have any Miracle Whip in the fridge?…If the neighbors' dog knocks over our trash cans again, I'm going to call them and give them a piece of my mind… ."

Such melodramas drain us of the inner energy we need for prayer and silent sitting, for growing inwardly and changing inwardly. The little melodramas of our lives are terrorists that kidnap our prayer-times and suck them dry of life! Each of us, if we pursued the raising of our spiritual consciousness, would find it to be the most exciting adventure and drama in the world. We do not need melodramas, nor can we afford to entertain them.

- 44 -

When we engage in them, we exaggerate the sticky areas of our interpersonal relationships and our other problems beyond their actual size. At the same time we blind ourselves to what is **really** necessary in the world. Melodramas prevent us from seeing the real necessity of our age: that we must become loving people who desire with a passion to be in communion with all people and with all of life. Melodramas keep our attention stuck on the surface of life: on overturned trash cans, half-baked potatoes and cold coffee. We thus easily overlook more meaningful inward realities.

If you wish to be part of the great cosmic spiritual leap forward, then do something! A contemporary poet, Marianne Moore, wrote,

> Hate-hardened heart, O heart of iron, iron is iron
> till it is rust.
> There never was a war that was not inward:
> I must fight till I have conquered in myself
> what causes war,
> But I would not believe it.
> I inwardly did nothing. O Iscariotlike crime!

Three Green Sprouts

Among the timeless fairy tales of old Europe is this delightful story:

A hermit who lived in a forest at the foot of a great mountain spent all his time in prayer and good works. Each evening he would carry, to the glory of God, two pails of water up the mountain to give drink to many a beast and plant. Living on that mountain at that time was a pack of terribly fierce birds which were dreaded by all who tried to climb the mountain. However, because the hermit was so prayerful, an angel of God, visible only to the hermit's eyes, would accompany him each time he climbed the mountain to protect him from the vicious birds. When he had finished his daily task of giving water to all the beasts and plants, the angel would bring him bread to eat. After many years of this service, it happened that one day, from far off, the old hermit saw a man being taken to the gallows. The usually kindly hermit thought, "There! That one is getting the just deserts for his crimes!"

That evening when he began to climb the mountain, no angel appeared to protect him. When he tried to carry his pails of water upward, the dreaded birds drove him back down the mountain. The hermit was confused. He prayed and fasted as he sought to understand what he had done to offend God.

After a month of penance, an angel came to his hermitage and said, "You have committed a grave injustice. You condemned a poor sinner who was being led to the gallows. That is why God is angry with you. Only God can judge another. However, if you do penance for your offense, you will once again know God's love." The hermit had forgotten all about his casual thought, and he begged to know what his penance would be.

"You must carry this lifeless branch," said the angel, handing him a dried-up twig, "until three green shoots sprout from it. And at night when you sleep, you must place it under your head. Further, you must leave this forest and beg for your bread from door to door. And you shall stay no more than one night in the same house."

So began the hermit's penance and return to the world. It was a hard life; many a door was slammed in his face. It was a life of hunger and rejection, for who likes a beggar? His wandering went on for years and years, but the branch remained lifeless. One night, after finding all doors closed to him, the hermit wandered into a forest until he came upon a cave. At its entrance sat a woman tending a pot of stew over an open fire. He begged her for some stew and a place to sleep. But she said to him, "Go away, old man, I do not dare feed you. I have three wicked and wild sons. They are robbers and have forbidden me to let anyone stop here. They will kill us both if they find that I have given you anything to eat or let you spend the night here. And they will return this very night, so be on your way!"

But the old man looked so exhausted that the woman's heart was moved to pity. So, against her better judgment she fed him and gave him a place to rest. As he prepared to go to sleep, she noticed the dead twig he placed under his head and asked about it. He told her the whole story of how one casual thought of judgment had separated him from God. The woman began to weep,

- 47 -

saying, "If this is God's punishment for one uncharitable thought, how will it fare with my three sons when they appear before God's throne?"

At midnight, her robber sons came home and saw the old man sleeping in the corner of the cave. They went into a rage at their mother who pleaded with them, "Let him be. He is only a poor sinner doing penance for his sins." The sons laughed and awakened the hermit, saying, "Tell us, old man, what crimes did **you** commit?"

So the old hermit told them the story of the mountain, the birds and his careless judgmental thought. Disarmed by the utter simplicity and sincerity of his story, they were deeply touched and were converted by his holiness. The next morning upon awakening, they found the old hermit dead. Under his head, the dead branch had grown three green sprouts.

Like the mother of the three sons, we too shudder at the idea of God being so displeased by a single casual thought of judgment. We wonder what penance we might deserve for all our judgmental thoughts. So often our heads become courthouses where the judge comes in, takes a peek through the door at those on trial and makes a rash judgment based solely on outward appearances. Then the judge takes his seat at the bench and goes through the charade of a trial that pretends all are innocent until proven guilty.

This tendency to prejudge, this prejudice, is a universal human failing. It is even reflected in the gospel story about the Canaanite woman who pleaded with Jesus to help her daughter. Jesus responded that his mission was to the people of Israel and that it wasn't fair to give the food of children to dogs (Mt. 15: 21-28). To the Jews of that time, the Canaanites were what native Americans were to many white settlers. Not that long ago there was a common saying: "The only good Indian is a dead one!" That's the way the Jews of Christ's time thought of Canaanites who, like our American Indians, had been the original inhabitants of their land. Conquered by the Israelites when they first came to Palestine, many Canaanites were killed. Others were forced into special areas, much like our Indian Reservations, and were treated with cruelty and disdain.

As Americans we have inherited the Anglo-Saxon notion of "fair play." We take pride in our legal system which guarantees a fair trial based solely on the evidence presented. We object strongly to the prejudgment of any citizen before his or her case is heard. Yet in our private lives we daily practice the very thing we would immediately reject in legal trials. We prejudge others on the basis of such externals as the color of their skin, their sex or their age. This habit of judging is also one of the major problems on the spiritual journey and is a main reason why our prayers, meditation and spiritual exercises tend to limp along half-heartedly or sink like a leaded balloon. But let's come back to that a bit later.

For now, I propose that we go on a little tour of our minds. Let's pay a visit to the courtroom of our consciousness. As if you were an outside observer, watch carefully as you mount the bench, put on the judge's solemn black robe and pass judgment without the benefit of evidence, defense or even a jury.

"Your honor, the following cases await your 'opinion':

> First: A young man and woman living together but not married—your judgment?
>
> Next: An elderly person slowly driving a car in front of yours?
>
> Next: A person of foreign origin speaking broken English?
>
> Next: A Jewish man or woman?
>
> Next: A black woman, unemployed with three children and on welfare?
>
> Next: A young woman with a beautiful child but never married?
>
> Next: A divorced man or woman?
>
> Next: Someone who has attempted suicide?
>
> Next: A black man and white woman dating one another?
>
> Next: A man who stays home, keeping house and raising the children while his wife goes to work?
>
> Next: A Moslem or Buddhist?

Next: An alcoholic or person who has had too much to drink?

Next: Someone who does not attend church on Sundays?

Next: A nun in full habit or still wearing a veil?

Next: Two men walking down the street holding hands?

Next: A military officer who is in charge of a nuclear missile silo?

Next: A priest who has married and is no longer functioning as a priest?...Someone dressed in a Neo-Nazi uniform with a Swastika armband?...Anti-nuclear demonstrators?...A woman employed at such 'man's' work as firefighting or construction work?..."

"Court dismissed!" Not because we have run out of cases for you to judge by a mere glance from your judge's chambers, but because we could go on for hours, and the point should be clear. How easily we sin as did the old man on the mountain. However, he learned by his pilgrimage of penance to see himself as neither better nor worse than others. He simply "saw" and made no judgments. Jesus obviously also "saw" the love of the Canaanite woman for her daughter and did not hold a judgment based on her tribe, caste or nation. In Jesus' own words: "Judge no one and you will not be judged" (Mt. 7:1).

It is our constant obsession with judging that creates so many problems in our prayer lives. We must never judge our prayer, especially meditation, as being good or bad, no matter how inspiring or dry it seems. We lack the ability to judge how God, to whom all prayer is directed, sees our feeble efforts. One of the most fundamental and important rules of the spiritual quest is: **Judge not your efforts to achieve holiness.** The only "bad" prayer is not to pray at all. We simply can say of our prayer time, "Well, today I had ten thousand and one distractions as I attempted to sit at my centering prayer"—period!

Such simple seeing is one of the aspects of childhood that we need to re-learn. In the process of becoming educated most of us lose that childlike sight that makes no judgment. We are continuously taught to analyze and evaluate. It requires humility just to let things be. We seem to need to make a judgment just to quiet our restless analytical minds which demand that NOTHING be left ambivalent. "Is it masculine or feminine? Is it good or bad? Is it easy or difficult?" True humility lets things be and allows us to simply be "at prayer," rather than labeling it as a "good" prayer or as a waste of time because it was full of distractions. Such humility, conversely, lets our prayer be all it can be.

We need a "pure vision" in order to be free of prejudice and to see things as they really are. In the *Svetasvatara Upanishad* of India it is said:

> May God...from whom all things come and into whom they all return, grant us the grace of pure vision. For You, O God, are the sun, the moon and the stars. You are the fire, the waters and the wind...You are this boy, and You are this maiden; You are this man and this woman; You are this old man who supports himself on a staff; You are the God who appears in forms in-finite!...When one knows God who is hidden in the heart of all, even as cream is hidden in milk, and in whose glory all things are, that person is free from all bondage.

Saint Paul has told us that we are "temples of the Holy Spirit"(1 Cor. 6: 19). Let us be temples then and not courthouses! If we are to be temples of God, then all that is in God should have a place of honor inside us. Perhaps the most important prayer for those seeking holiness is not adoration, meditation or praise but the daily prayer of cultivating pure vision, a prayer of cleansing and demolishing! Daily we must sweep out the courtroom from our mind. Daily we must take a crowbar and sledge hammer to the courthouse that keeps supplanting the temple of God that is our body. Throw out the judge, black robe and all, so that you may see "God who appears in forms infinite...God who is hidden in the heart of all." Be prepared, however, that this is not a once-in-a-lifetime revolution but rather a constant cleansing of the inner house of prayer.

We should also recall the good advice of St. Paul: "It matters little to me whether you or any human court pass judgment on me. I do not even pass judgment on myself. God is the one to judge me"(1 Cor. 4: 3). The most difficult penance we can undertake, worse than the itchiest hair shirt, is the spiritual discipline of "only seeing." How hard it is to simply make the observation, "I see that John does not go to church," refusing to let a trial and judgment take place. Such refusal to judge, like all virtues, begins with ourselves. Like St. Paul, we must even refuse to pass judgment on ourselves, our prayers, our attempts to be saintly or our efforts to be in communion with God. We need to suspend such self-judgment in order to let God come through to us.

Of course, the Church too needs to cultivate "pure vision." It needs to restrain the tendency to make judgments about the quality of our relationships with God or our communion—or lack of it—with the rest of the Body of Christ. We, as the Church, need to live out, as well as teach, the attitude of Jesus toward the woman who was about to be stoned for being caught in an act of sin. After he had told the crowd that the one who had not committed sin should cast the first stone, they all dispersed. And Jesus told the woman, "Is there no one left to condemn you? Then neither will I" (Jn. 8: 1-11).

I would close this reflection about another way to "love yourself with all your heart and love your neighbor as yourself," another way "to see the Rabbit," with this suggestion. Go outside and pick up a barren dead twig. Bring it inside and place it in your prayer corner, on your family altar, on your desk or your kitchen window sill. Let it be a powerful mini-sacramental, a religious icon. Let it be a reminder as you travel on your spiritual path, just as it was for the old hermit. And if, like him, you do your best not to judge others, at your death they can place the twig in your hands. I assure you that it will have bloomed with at least three green shoots and will be your ticket to paradise.

Finding God Outside the Law

Once, many years ago, there was a traditional Saturday wedding in the ageless small town of Canaville, Kentucky. The late-morning ceremony was followed by the usual wedding dance in the town's only hall. Everyone in Canaville and many of the surrounding hill-country folk were present. The wedding dance was still in full swing well into the night as young and old alike were stomping out to the beat of the three-piece band. When the clock on the wall of the dance hall read 11:45 P.M., a sudden sour note was struck. The manager of the hall called the groom aside and said to him, "It's 11:45...remember, we close in fifteen minutes!"

The groom and other members of the wedding party objected, "Come on, Jake. Why the party's only started! Look, everyone is having the time of their lives."

The manager only shook his head, "We **have** to close at midnight—county law, you know. And in fifteen minutes, gents, it'll be Sunday! This is a God-fearin', law-abidin' Christian county. So we close up at twelve sharp. That's the Law!"

A heaviness fell upon the wedding dance as if someone had turned out the lights. But just when it seemed like the feasting was about to flicker out, something happened to transform the gloom in the town hall. Among the guests at the wedding was a tall stranger from a little town up north of Canaville. His mother came over to him with this request, "Son, it would be a shame for this dance to have to end simply because it'll be Sunday in fifteen minutes. Can't you do something, please?"

After a short pause to consider the situation, the stranger slowly raised his arm and pointed his index finger at the clock on the wall of the dance hall. Astonishingly, the hands on that old clock began to move backwards—as did the hands on every watch in the dance hall and on every clock in Canaville! Soon all the clocks read 11:44, then 11:43, and then 11:42 as time passed.

It was the longest, most enjoyable wedding dance that anyone, regardless of age, could remember. Everyone was delighted—everyone, that is, except the pious churchgoers and the three pastors of the town's churches, because Sunday never came! That weekend there was no Sunday. Instead there were two Saturdays, and then it was Monday!

The little Kentucky town of Canaville was split down the middle. Some town-folk were guilt-ridden because they hadn't gone to church on Sunday, and some were tickled to death because they didn't have to go—because that week "there weren't no Sunday."

Right about now, I'll bet you're thinking that this sounds a lot like another wedding, the famous gospel wedding of Cana. Unlike the Gospel story, however, not everyone was pleased with the miracle at the Canaville wedding. Yet, who knows? Perhaps everyone wasn't pleased as punch with the one at Cana either!

Jesus, at the beginning of his public life, revealed himself as a liberator. While everyone in Israel longed and looked for a messianic savior who would free them from political oppression and foreign occupation, this wasn't the kind of liberator that Jesus chose to be. And that began to be clear when he appeared in the little town of Cana not simply as a guest and miracle-worker but also as a new kind of liberator.

When told that the party would end because they had run out

of wine (a Palestinian wedding would collapse into a wake without *the* sign of joy and celebration: wine!), Jesus went to the waiters. He gave them strange instructions, telling them to put water not into the wine bottles—or in this case the wine skins—but into stone water jars! We are told in the Gospels that the water in those stone jars was intended exclusively for ritual hand washing. The effect of the miracle was not just to produce 150 gallons of wine. It also made the ritualistic hand washing impossible, that is, unless the devout wanted to wash their hands in wine!

One of the strict religious obligations of devout Jews was the washing of hands before and after each meal, and after each course of a meal. This washing was performed as a precise ritual: one hand was washed first, and then the water dripped down into the other. Then the fist of the first hand was rubbed in the palm of the second while certain prescribed prayers were recited.

If Jesus solved one problem at the wedding of Cana, he surely created a second and bigger dilemma. Picture in your mind people—especially the pious and legalistic—walking around at the wedding feast, saying, "Where's the water to wash our hands?" Some must have been squirming in a sea of scruples, while others, perhaps, were dancing with delight because the means of fulfilling their obligation had disappeared!

Organized religion and its laws and rituals are intended to be a means to more easily know, love and serve God. But how easily prayer, worship and religion **become** God. Religious practice can become an end-in-itself, or at least more important than real charity. The Jewish hand-washing ritual was intended to raise consciousness about the sacredness of meals. But in practice it only locked people into a consciousness of the need to clean their hands. As with any other religious law—like going to church on Sunday—it often blocked an awareness of the living reality of God.

Religious rituals, spiritual disciplines and worship can imprison us when, "come hell or high water," they **must** be performed. When nothing can replace a religious duty, then we have invested that observance with godhood. When we do not love ourselves as we should, we need signs that we are lovable, even by God.

For many of us, at least at certain times, being strict about keeping religious duties gives proof that we are good, God-fearing and devout.

Jesus, at Cana, removed the necessity and even the possibility of performing a religious obligation. By transforming water, the substance of fulfilling that obligation, into wine, the symbol of joy, Jesus was making a strong statement. Perhaps we could express his message in these words: "I have come not to destroy laws and rituals but to rescue them and you! See, I liberate laws and transform them into acts of joy."

This type of liberation isn't restricted to pious oppression. For we can also easily become ensnared in a web of personal rituals and rigid patterns of behavior. Daily routines and legalisms, like vampires, can suck the very life and joy out of our lives. In government, business, schools and our homes, when it comes to laws and routines, none are free of the potential for this kind of deadening enslavement. How readily do we make ourselves victims of compulsive rituals and duties that take precedent over human needs and even over life itself! It is easy to laugh at the superstitions of primitive peoples, but our word "superstition" is a child of the Latin mother-word *superstare* which literally means, "stand over." Any ritual or routine holds a godlike power over us when it towers high and oppresses us with the command, "This must be done!"

All life, whether in the larger society or at home, has its rules. For life without laws seems beyond our present state of evolution. Laws are necessary when there is an absence of mature love. From civil laws to "whose-turn-is-it-to-do-the-dishes?" our days are filled with regulations because of a lack of real respect for ourselves and others. It is clear that Church laws about divorce are of concern only to those who have "fallen" out of love. And if we had a loving concern for all children, we would slow down to a crawl, without traffic laws, when driving past schools or areas where children play. Traffic laws are necessary because we tend to be concerned only with our personal agendas, our own "urgent" needs and pleasures.

Those who call themselves disciples of Jesus are invited to

follow the example of their spiritual master, who announced that the reign of God had appeared! The "good news" is that goodness is **not** found in the keeping of complex, if not compulsive, religious laws. Rather, goodness is hidden inside the most ordinary of everyday activities. And for Jesus to proclaim what liberation meant, he, first of all, had to know the escape hatch from the Bastille of Blessed Laws.

A true leader is not one who holds power over others but one who **leads**, who does first what he or she desires others to do. So let's look again at the wedding of Cana. The water jars were in place at that wedding because every feast had them—it was the law. Jesus stepped out on a legal limb and posed, in a quiet way, an important question: "Are these **really** necessary?" He was able to raise this question because he had already cut through to what is essential. He had found a way of living that was free and yet totally aligned with what is true and good. Jesus, during his family life in Nazareth, had learned that goodness is not found in following stringent observances. It is not found in walking the socially correct path. We are invited to learn that the Good, that which gives birth to happiness, can be found in doing even the most ordinary things of life with a wholeness of heart, a wholeness of attention.

Being a disciple of Christ requires looking carefully at our personal habits and rituals. Daily routines of when and how we brush our teeth or how we begin our day can make life flow more easily. The thousand little rituals of our personal lives allow us to move through the day without having to plan or think about everything we do. However, while we are in the midst of the ritual of washing the dishes or a ritual act of worship—anything that is done out of habit—our minds are often busy with other thoughts.

Living mindfully, investing all of life with a love that is expressed with a full heart, mind, soul and body, frees us from the prison of preoccupation. We can see, hear, feel, taste and touch the fleeting moment of life that is passing through our fingers. Life is a gift whose ultimate purpose is pleasure. If we are to fully enjoy life, we cannot sleepwalk our way through it. If we are to taste and smell the fragrance of God, if we are to delight in the Wedding Feast to which Christ invites us, we must remain alert and awake. Those who are awake, who are mindful, find that they live inside a perpetual miracle, an ongoing wedding feast. The miracle is that common, ordinary water can taste like the finest vintage wine if we drink it with mindfulness, savoring its delicate taste, its refreshing wetness.

As the Arch-liberator, Jesus would have agreed with Chairman Mao and Karl Marx that revolution is a constant occupation. Each celebration of a revolution, whether it be the Fourth of July, Bastille Day or the wedding feast at Cana should remind us that we are in the midst of a revolution. We need that mindfulness if we wish to live in the "glorious freedom of the children of God" (Rom. 8: 21). We must constantly keep turning away from the slavery of self, from the slavish observance of any ritual act, personal or religious. If the Way, if one's spiritual path, is to be filled with joy and delight, then it must be free of all "superstitious" duties, rituals and routines. When we break our habits, when we become free of habitual ways of being, we can break open the kernel of joy present in every act. For at each moment and in every action, the Divine Reality resides. Even a casual reading of the behavior of Jesus of Nazareth reveals a man who always put religious laws in second place—and the love of God, neighbor and self first!

Reflecting on this, however, do not forget that our Leader was "properly dealt with" for being a revolutionary (the charge leveled against him at his trial). Remember too that he promised that if we truly follow him, we should expect the same treatment. There is, of course, an "easy" solution to such a sticky problem: do not follow the Leader but instead only worship him. Yet it is only by celebrating and participating in a revolution such as Jesus led that we can break through to a new level of being. It is only then that we really encounter the Divine and begin to celebrate a wedding feast without any clocks!

The Fine Wine of Commitment

We should not be surprised to find a bank at the head of a list of the twelve oldest businesses in the world! The Assyrian Bank of Egibi & Son has been in continuous operation since 700 B.C. Others on that list, however, might not be as obvious. Seven of those businesses are involved in the production of beverages. The second and third places are occupied by Bavarian breweries which have been in continuous operation since 1040 A.D. and 1119 A.D. respectively. Five others on that famous list are French and German vineyards.

While it is not included among the twelve, marriage might have been listed as one of the oldest businesses. Historically, society has looked upon marriage as a business, as a means of acquiring money, property and possessions. The Western custom of "marrying for love" is a rather recent development in the evolution of that old institution. In Israel of long ago, marriage contracts were not made between the bride and groom but between two families. Marriage was an exchange of property, and the relationship of the groom and bride reflected this fact. The Hebrew name for groom was *Ba'al*, which means "owner," and the name for bride was *Beulah*, meaning "owned."

But marriage is not so much like a business as a bottle of wine. A good marriage is like a bottle of 1947 Lafite Rothschild. If you could find a bottle of that vintage, it would be worth several thousand dollars! In fact, a bottle of Lafite Rothschild Bordeaux of the year 1806 recently sold for $28,000. A Rothschild Bordeaux of 1959 or earlier is a marvelously aged blend of sugar and acid.

Not every wine, however, improves with age. Most wines should not be "laid down" (that is, stored away for years) but should be drunk within a few years after they have been bottled. If you fail to drink many wines soon, they will not only lack quality, they will turn sour. But a good French Bordeaux needs time to acquire greatness. The secret of a truly fine bottle of wine lies in the correct balance of sweetness and fruity acidity. Its greatness is only acquired in time, although you can drink a fine wine when it is "young," and it will have a delightful flavor. That early sweetness might be compared to the delights of romance in the beginning of a relationship.

With the passage of years, however, good wine matures, and all sorts of subtle scents and delightful flavors emerge. The first sweetness gives way to an oily richness with the suggestion of countless flowers, herbs, fruits and spices. The same is true for any human relationship, whether a marriage, friendship or bond between a person and a religious community. Every relationship is a mixture of sugar and acid, of good and bad, joy and suffering, all within the blending of two different personalities. When those two personalities are united within the context of a commitment, they can mature to a great richness like that of an old Lafite Rothschild. What makes that Bordeaux such a treat is that the wine has remained corked in the same bottle for so many years. Similarly, it is permanence, fidelity and the commitment to find a balance that create the masterpiece of a fine relationship.

The life story of a bottle of Bordeaux is a parable that can teach us the essential element in any relationship. It is the sense of commitment that finds its expression in the words of the marriage ceremony: "until death do us part." Many people today see those words as a threat to freedom. Some couples have removed the phrase altogether, while others have changed it to "as long as our love shall last." We know that Christ's call to a lifelong commitment in marriage was a call to perfection. He presented us with the ideal. Marriage, to Jesus, was the great sign of the unconditional commitment between God and the world. But the ideal was not always possible. Indeed, Jesus presented us with many ideals in his summons to perfection. There is the challenge to live in a poverty which places its dependence not upon bank accounts but totally upon the providence of God. There is the call to a perfection of love which includes the ideal of total nonviolence, of never returning injury for injury. Even the most superficial look at history shows that Christian people have frequently been unable to live up to such demanding standards.

Perhaps some marriages, like some wines, lack the necessary elements to remain united and to mature into a work of art like a fine wine. Perhaps some marriages, like some wines, turn to vinegar if they are "laid down" for many years. Both fine wines and fine marriages require the right choice of ingredients. More than simple attraction is necessary for greatness in any relationship.

However, once a life-choice is made, commitment is essential. Such a commitment cannot simply be "for the sake of the children" or because "we have promised." It must be a commitment to developing the depth and greatness of human love. When people say, "until death do us part," what are they really promising? Can anyone really promise what will be in the future? Who can foresee the numerous changes in values and attitudes that will unfold with the passage of years? Is it not even possible that God might repeat history and call one to "leave husband or wife, children and family" (Lk. 14:26)? None of us can promise what we will do in the future. The expression "until death do us part" is a ritual, coded expression. It can be translated, "I will do my very best, my damndest, to make this union truly great." Now that is a promise one can keep—not easily, but it can be kept!

Life commitments in marriage, friendship or religious life should always be viewed backwards! They are like rings on a tree stump. As long as the tree is vital and alive, it adds another ring each year. As we make new commitments to life together, one by one, the rings grow until we can count 18, 25, 34 or 58 years. The same creative maturing process goes on inside a bottle of Bordeaux. It continues to grow in richness as long as the process inside the bottle remains creative. So marriages and friendships can withstand wars and storms, economic depressions and hard times, misunderstandings and even infidelities. Anything can be weathered as long as there exists in that union the unfolding of creative life and love. That unfolding love involves a continual opening of self to the other and a deep desire that the relationship remain mutually enriching.

If you could be given the opportunity to slip behind the cork of a bottle of fine wine, you would sense this "commitment" between the sugar and acid. There is an inherent "pledge" that the two will remain together even during the occasional unpleasantness of the chemical interaction between them. It is as if they were saying, "Let's stay together and keep working for the perfect balance; let's stay together to create greatness." It is this greatness of love that was the hope of Jesus. Marriage was not a business to him, not an arrangement about property. It was to be a sign of the Kingdom.

While the institution of marriage has come a long way since the arranged "business marriages" of long ago, human relationship is still sometimes regarded as a type of ownership. For many couples, "fidelity" in marriage is often only a form of "exclusive rights," a way of legally saying, "You belong to me." Such a view is only a one-way street to the vice of jealousy. Fidelity in a relationship more truly lies in a faith in each other. It is a belief that each partner holds the ability to call forth the best from the other. It is a faith in each other's uniqueness, hidden potential and gifts. Such a belief in the loved one is foremost a faith in the power of love to fulfill the promise of that potential. Unfortunately a vast number of marriages and relationships are destroyed by infidelity. That infidelity, however, is often not so much an alliance with a third party as a lack of believing deeply in the other. When deep love-faith is absent, greatness cannot be achieved, no matter how long the relationship lasts!

All love begins with the intoxicating feeling of singularity: "You are the only one for me!" But as love matures and grows toward greatness, that singularity should open up, unfolding into a universal sense of oneness. Mature love should open us to a loving unity with God, the world and all creation. Such a love involves freedom with responsibility. Indeed, all life commitments include struggle. On occasion such struggles can be difficult and painful; the same is true for the creative tension within a bottle of fine wine. Yet, without struggle in our relationships, our love will lack the dynamism, the critical mass of energy, necessary to create the Kingdom and heal the world—or even to make us happy. It thus becomes clear that in a society where commitments can easily be dissolved whenever there is struggle, fruitful marriage and friendship are in danger.

As this reflection concludes, remember that God has chosen human love as the sacrament and sign of the Divine Love. Your love, therefore, possesses great power. God will fuel your love with all the grace and energy necessary to resolve the occasional struggles that are part of any maturing process. Believe deeply in the other person—or in your community. Your fidelity, furthermore, has the power to call forth from the other a belief in you, in your uniqueness and potential. A whole and healthy love is of far greater value than any bottle of Lafite Rothschild, regardless of its age. Our world is thirsty for the mature wine of great love. Who does not dance inwardly when given the privilege of relishing an expression of mature love? What a gift it is when others share with us the intoxicating result of many years of affectionate fidelity. That sort of mature love heals the world, lifts our hearts and renews our belief in the unconditional and passionate love of our God.

The Search for Truth

In all the great religions of the world we encounter the importance of being committed to the truth. From the prayer of the scriptures of India, "From the unreal lead me to the truth" to the prayer of Jesus that his disciples would be "consecrated in the truth" (Jn. 17: 19), each great spiritual path stresses a dedication to truth. Jesus also promised that his disciples would know the truth and that "the truth will set you free" (Jn. 8: 32). Each year on Good Friday the primacy of the truth comes into focus when we hear the exchange between Jesus the Nazarene and Pilate the politician. Jesus says that his purpose in life is to "testify to the truth," and Pilate answers, "Truth! What does that mean?" (Jn. 18: 37).

We live in an age of massive political cover-ups. And although Vietnam and Watergate can seem lifetimes ago, something like the Iranian arms deal always seems to pop up. It's become easy to suspect that not only the used car salesman but perhaps even our president will engage in untruths and withhold information. In such an age, maintaining a personal dedication to the truth is certainly difficult. You and I believe, as our Lord tells us, that the truth will set us free. However, we also know from personal experience how painful truth can be, even when we know it to be liberating. The demands of kindness, for example, can convince us to set aside truth in order to "spare the feelings" of another.

You wouldn't be reading this if you didn't have some commitment to the spiritual quest. So I expect that you will acknowledge that a reflection on truth cannot be avoided at some point, no matter how much we may skirt it in our daily lives. How easily we can lie to others and to ourselves. Yet when we lie to ourselves about our addictions or our true feelings, we can literally make ourselves sick. So perhaps Pilate's question isn't so cynical after all. In fact, the question, "What is truth?" is essential to the spiritual journey. Here is a story about a search for truth that may help us explore that question:

> Once upon a time, a certain successful man became restless. He told his wife, "Although I am rich and successful, I am not happy. More than anything else in life, I desire to know the truth. I must leave you, the children and my work to go out and search for truth."
>
> His wife was most understanding. She loved him and realized that her happiness was intimately connected with her husband's. She encouraged his quest, and within days, after making sure that his family's needs were taken care of, he was gone. He wandered the earth for years, visiting gurus and gray-bearded scholars. He climbed holy mountains, visited temples and shrines and questioned mystics. But he did not find the truth.
>
> After many long years he met a holy man who told him that on a certain mountain in a far-distant land he would find the truth. With great eagerness, anticipating that his long quest was about to end, he traveled to the far-off land and climbed the difficult mountain. At the very top he came to a dark cave. There, sitting at the cave's entrance, was the ugliest woman he had ever seen. She was an old hag, with one lone tooth hanging from her aged gums. Her skin was like yellowed newspaper, and her dirty hair hung in oily strings over her stooped, bony shoulders. She looked out at him from eyes sunk in deep pockets in her skull, buried in concentric circles

of purple flesh. "Well," she snarled, "what do you want here?"

The seeker replied, "I am here after a long and difficult journey that has taken years. I have come seeking the truth!"

Motioning to him with a crooked, bony finger, she led him back into the damp darkness of the mountain. In the blackness of the cave she began to speak—and her voice was the most beautiful he had ever heard. He **knew** he had found the truth!

For a year he lived with her in the cave, and she taught him what no guru or scholar could teach. She taught him the truth. When the year was almost over and he was preparing to return to his family and the world, he asked, "What can I do to thank you for this most precious treasure which you have given me?"

Hesitantly, she leaned forward and whispered into his ear, "When your people ask about me, tell them...that I was beautiful!"

Aha! What, indeed, is the truth? Is truth different for the trial judge than for the shaman or spiritual master? Is truth a different experience for a Greek, an Indian or an Anglo-Saxon? When Jesus spoke of truth, he did so as a Hebrew, or at least through that cultural prism. The old Hebrew word for truth is more correctly a concept of reality than of informational correctness, as it is in our Anglo-Saxon heritage. The *true* was understood as the *real*. Unlike a lie, which is unreality, the true is that in which one can put one's faith. That is so because reality is worthy of trust, and God is the ultimate reality or truth in which to place one's trust. The truth, then, in Jesus' cultural background, is not something to which one gives intellectual assent. It is rather something to which one gives a deeply personal commitment. So when the ancients spoke of a *true God*, they meant a *real* God. We come close to this notion of the truth when we speak of a *true* friend. A real friend will remain faithful regardless of the winds of ill fortune or clouds of negative public opinion. No matter what you do or what happens to you, such a friend will not desert you.

Our life journey is a quest for the True as expressed in the beautiful Hindu prayer, "From illusion, lead me to the truth." At the conclusion of experiences that take us higher or deeper than everyday life, we often say something like, "Well, now I have to get back to the real world." Paradoxically, however, such profoundly spiritual experiences are **very** real, or true, because they approach the eternal. What we commonly call the "real" world is actually a passing and transitional one. The purpose of the spiritual quest is to be cured of the blindness that prevents us from seeing and knowing what is truly real and what is not.

Jesus said that the gift of his body and blood was true food and real drink. How about hamburgers and coffee—are they true food and drink? Mystical food provides true nourishment because it is eternal: it is beyond time and decay. The food and drink of this world only mirrors the lasting food. As you reflect on the riddle of what is lasting and true, you might again think about the parable of the old hag in the cave. Did she really tell the man to lie? Or was she really beautiful, with a beauty which never fades? Which woman did he encounter during that year in the cave—the one visible to his natural eyes or the one which he saw with the eyes of his heart? Ah, yes, Pilate's question is beginning to make more sense with each passing minute.

Pilate, that political-and-social climber, lived in a time as difficult as ours. Like Pilate, we live in an age of transition, where old social forms have lost their original power and have begun to crumble while new ones begin to rise. This is the end of the industrial age, and as the institutions of industrial society are swaying on their foundations, we long for concrete values. Even such traditionally strong structures as the institutions of marriage, the family, school and religion are on shaky ground. In such an age, the hunger for certitude is great.

The sudden rise of fundamentalism, especially in Christianity and Islam, is not surprising. In all forms of fundamentalism we see what Juan-Lorenzo Hinjojosa calls a "lust for certainty." In this time of confusion people crave **absolute** truths. They want the Bible to be "true"—literally—every word and story. There is no room for uneasy questions about evolution—or an evolutionary morality. Scripture must be unquestioned not only spiritually but historically and biologically as well. Some people lust after dogmas and absolute moral laws that are so sharp in their definition that the contrast between black and white hurts the eyes. They long for the Church to dictate what is moral and what is not.

As we move into the twenty-first century, those voices crying out for certainty grow louder and louder. Many religions claim to be the one "true" religion of God. Each one declares that its scriptures are the true and last word of God. This form of lust after ultimate authority is not new, even though its present expression is so vocal. Yet does it seem consistent with the way of the living Truth that God would have said everything we need to hear some two or three thousand years ago? Does it not seem true—consonant with the Divine Nature—that the one God would continue to speak to us in a variety of "voices" and in a variety of ways? Does it not seem true that Divine Revelation would use world events as well as the personal experiences of our lives as sources by which a living God could continue to lead us as Abraham or Jesus were led?

Part of the pain of being a spiritual seeker is that one must live without certainty. Part of the price of being a disciple of Truth and a lover of union involves embracing the suffering of doubt. For is it certainty or questioning that brings us closer together? A character in Graham Green's *Msgr. Quixote* says, "It's odd how a showing of doubt can bring men together even more than a sharing of faith. The believer will fight another believer over a shade of difference; the doubter fights only within himself... ." The ancient search for Truth is not a journey toward certitude but toward timeless realities. A real seeker after the Truth looks for it in every situation.

As disciples of Truth we need to accept the reality that we will be seekers more than possessors of truth. We cannot invest ourselves in the appearance of things but rather in what promises lasting value. A pilgrim of reality has different values and thus finds happiness in places that seldom appear in full-color advertisements. And to these, one more discipline should be added: that we always try our best to speak the truth. As we take on this last challenge, we must realize that it is the most complex. A friend who is a country attorney in a small Kansas town told me this story:

> Once, in the middle of a jury trial, an old farmer was asked by the judge to swear on the Bible that he would tell the whole truth and nothing but the truth. The farmer flat refused. When the judge asked him why, he answered, "Well, your honor, in the first place I don't know if I know the whole truth. And even if I knew the whole truth, I wonder if you or the jury could stand to hear it. So, if you don't mind, your honor, I'll tell you as much of the truth as I think I know and as much as I think you and the jury can bear to hear."

My friend said that the judge smiled and let the farmer testify under those conditions. A wise man, that farmer. When we think we know the "whole" truth, how little we actually know. Part of a dedication to speaking truly also involves deciding how well our part of the truth can be heard and embraced by others. We need to keep in mind, however, that while this decision is difficult, most studies show that the problem is more our fear of speaking the truth than the inability of others to hear it. Most people can bear more truth than we think they can tolerate. So as disciples of Truth we must be willing to enter that arena of self-wrestling and prepared to come out of such a contest always a little unsure.

Finally, as we willingly take upon ourselves the various struggles connected with the spiritual quest, we can also rejoice that true happiness is found in the real things of life. The further we journey on as pilgrims of Truth, the less we are thrown off course by our hardships and pain and the more our sense of joy radiates. Part of the joy of the quest is the delight we experience when the Real shines out like a pearl from the persons and events of our lives. I'd like to conclude this reflection with one last story:

> Once, long ago, a boy in Tibet went on a pilgrimage to the great shrine of the Buddha at Lhasa. His mother

could not go with him so she asked him to bring her back a relic from the shrine. Now the journey to the shrine was a great and colorful adventure for the boy. The shrine itself was overwhelming in its golden beauty. In his excitement the boy forgot about his promise to his mother until he was on his way home, less than a mile outside his village. He looked around frantically for something, anything, that he might bring her. Spying the bones of a dead dog along the side of the road, he picked up one of the dog's teeth. He wrapped the tooth in a silk cloth and took it home. Presenting it to his mother, he said, "Here, mother, is a relic of the Buddha from his shrine."

Happily the mother took the tooth and placed it reverently in a place of honor on the small altar in her home. She prayed before it each day with great devotion.

One day the tooth began to glow with a soft light. Soon the entire village began coming to her home to worship at the Shrine of the Holy Tooth. Numerous cures and miracles took place there, to the great pride of the boy's mother. In fact, the only thing the woman could talk about was the miraculous powers of the Buddha's tooth, the wonders worked before her relic.

After years of this the young man grew tired of his mother's pious talk. One day he shouted at her, "Mother, stop it! That's only a tooth from a dead dog that I found beside the road outside our village."

But his mother would have none of it and replied, "You are mistaken, son. The truth is that this is a great and holy relic of the Lord Buddha."

Angry at her unyielding persistence, the young man stormed out of the house only to run directly into the Lord Buddha himself standing on the doorstep. Solemnly the Buddha said to him, "That tooth, my son, is **truly** one of mine!"

Holy ⚲ Hypocrisy

One of the secrets of holiness lies hidden in hypocrisy. That may sound like a strange statement since holiness and hypocrisy seem to be as opposed to each other as war and peace! But perhaps a reflection on masks and their colorful and varied use can help us see how hypocrisy and holiness are interrelated.

The history of masks is truly prehistoric. In many lands and among diverse peoples, the mask has been considered a magical and religious object. It was an important part of sacred drama, which began not so much as entertainment as worship. In fact, the first theater in the Western world was located in a church—the shrine of Dionysus at Athens. Dressed as gods, the priests or their assistants performed dramatic plays wearing masks of the divine ones. With the passage of time, the theater lost its religious grounding. Even so, actors continued to wear masks, portraying virtues like courage and honesty and vices like jealousy and rage. Nevertheless, despite that long and honored tradition, the Western theater today makes use of masks only rarely.

On the other hand, masks are frequently employed in our society by terrorists or bank robbers, who use them to hide their real identity. This wearing of masks is for an evil and immoral purpose. Masks, however, can also hide a person's identity for a noble purpose. Such larger-than-life characters as the Lone

Ranger, Batman and Spiderman wear masks in their efforts to defeat evil. The classic half-mask they wear is called a *domino*. It was first used around 1500 by clowns in Italy to entertain and amuse and only later became the disguise of heroes like Zorro and the Lone Ranger. So wearing a mask to hide one's identity can be a good thing. Jesus, however, didn't agree with that statement—or at least he didn't seem to.

Over and over in the Gospels we find Jesus thundering out against hypocrites, against those who wear masks. "When you give alms, for example, do not blow a horn before you in synagogues and streets like hypocrites looking for applause" (Mt. 6: 12). "When you are praying, do not behave like the hypocrites...on street corners in order to be noticed" (Mt. 6: 5). "Woe to you scribes and Pharisees, you hypocrites" (Mt. 23: 13). The word *hypocrite* originally meant an actor. In ancient Greece it referred to an actor who wore a mask. A hypocrite, as Jesus used the word, is one who pretends, one who wears a thin mask of artificial goodness to disguise the darkness and sin within. Jesus exposed his wrath against those who pretend to pray or be holy but on the inside—in reality—are full of malice and evil thoughts. He leveled those charges against the religiously pious people of his day. Today, ironically, those who are non-religious often accuse practicing Christians of the same charge—of being hypocrites! They accuse churchgoers of only pretending to be prayerful, of only play-acting at worship, while all the time overflowing with gossip, slander, uncharitable thoughts, petty division, prejudice and hate.

If we are honest, we must confess that such a charge is not totally unfounded. If you were seeking a truly generous person, someone who is kind, caring, open to change and free from discrimination, would you go to church to find such a person? How often do we find that those who call themselves religious, devout churchgoers are actually narrow, bigoted, uncompassionate, rigid resisters to any real change of heart?

Benjamin Hill, in his tribute to the great Southern general, wrote of Robert E. Lee:

> He was a foe without hate, a friend without treachery,
> a soldier without cruelty, and a victim without murder-
> ing. He was a public officer without vices, a private
> citizen without wrong, a neighbor without reproach, a
> Christian without hypocrisy, and a man without guile.

A man without a mask, without deceit, so it seems, was the great Robert E. Lee. Am I such a person of integrity? At my funeral, will they say of me what Hill said of General Lee? "He was a Christian without hypocrisy."

Are you a hypocrite? Do you wear a mask? Are you one person at work, another at home; one person at the golf course or in a bar and another in church? Yes, I expect you are—and so am I! We all wear masks and play roles which we either choose or are forced into by society. Yes, we are all hypocrites. Masking the truth was a talent we first learned at our mother's knee. One of the earliest lessons we learned from our parents, right after toilet training, was hypocrisy. When Aunt Nellie came to visit, we looked at her and said something like, "Aunt Nellie, what a big nose you have!" As soon as auntie left, we were dutifully instructed that such honesty was neither kind nor polite. These were followed by other lessons. "The dinner was wonderful," when in reality it was bland. "We had a grand time," when we were really bored. We learned to be gentlemen and gentlewomen who practiced the art of hypocrisy so as not to offend. Such acts of "consideration" can easily produce a "domino" effect of hypocrisy.

One of my earliest lessons I remember well: "Edward, be a gentleman. A gentleman never causes pain to others." So it may be that there can be good hypocrisy and bad hypocrisy. If that is true, then there can be good masks as well as bad masks, even if we aren't super-heroes-or-heroines. Who knows, maybe all life is one long Halloween where we wear costumes and masks that hide our real selves or the undeveloped parts of our personalities. But how can hypocrisy, the wearing of a false face, ever be good? Perhaps a story can help reveal how there can be such a thing as a "good" hypocrite.

Once upon a time there lived a man whose face was terribly deformed. His countenance was truly horrible to look upon and people avoided the sight of him. Since people tend to look upon that which is beautiful or handsome as good and that which is ugly and horrible as bad, people thought of him as evil. And so he was forced to live a lonely life.

One day the deformed man went to an old mask maker and asked him to construct the mask of a saint. The old man was truly an artist and created a mask so lifelike that no one suspected that it was not the deformed man's real face. He wore the mask day and night, whether at home or away. Because he looked like a saint, people expected him to act like one. The man tried to play the part as best he could. After a time, a good and lovely woman fell in love with him and became his constant companion. One day she discovered that he was wearing a mask and asked him to remove it. He was afraid of losing her affection, and so he refused time and again to take the mask off. Finally she convinced him that her love was strong enough to withstand any sight. So, with misgivings, he removed the mask. She stared at him in shock—in utter bewilderment—and said, "Why do you wear that mask? Your face is exactly the same as the mask!" The actor had **become** the role he played!

Fake it until you make it

Saints are the heroes and the heroines of the inner life, and we need them today more than ever. Perhaps we should all go to some master mask maker and have a mask of a saint made to fit our face. As holy hypocrites, then, we would wear the mask night and day, striving at all times to live and act as if we were saints. The result? In time we would very likely become saints!

There is, unfortunately, no such thing as the mask of a saint, no real saint that is. A mask is a face set in one fixed position, one frozen attitude. Holiness, on the other hand, has ten thousand faces! The problem with the plaster saints that stand silently in our churches or which piously smile at us from picture frames is that they all have the very same face. They all have a "saintly" countenance: pious, detached, serene, without move-

ment or elasticity. The real saint's expression is a flowing experience: now compassionate, now angry, now sad, now joyful, now strong, now gentle and caring. As a holy person comes closer to complete union with the Divine Mystery, he or she becomes more fluid, more elastic, more free to express the full spectrum of divine qualities. The paradox is that the more one becomes absorbed in the One, the more individual, unique and creative one becomes.

Each time we worship, we are involved in a sacred drama. This drama is also a masquerade, where all who attend wear a mask. The mask we wear, like those in the early Greek theater, is a godly image. It is the image of who we are called to be, not a disguise to hide who we think we are. It is important to make a distinction between wearing a mask to appear holy and wearing a mask to become holy. Yet, worry about the gap between who-you-are and the holy who-you-appear-to-be only if there is no desire, no daily effort to become a better person. A person who seeks with a passion to become Christlike is a good hypocrite.

Perhaps the only way we shall become saints is the same way that the deformed man in the story changed his appearance. The trick of transformation lies in how we live our lives. We become what we pretend to be. Let us go forth from worship or prayer wearing the mask of a saint and trying to act like one. From dawn to dusk, climbing into bed and getting out of bed, in every place and at all times, we can live as if we were the person whose image is on the mask we wear. We can be like the original Greek hypocrites with the hope that when we die and they lift off our "holy" mask, they will find beneath it the face of holiness.

saints
Reminds me of a joke
How to tell difference
between saint + a martyr

Discovering the Grace of Disgrace

While we seek grace from God at every turn, there is one kind of grace we avoid like the thought of AIDS. It speaks of a simplicity of spirit that even those who have embraced total poverty of possessions are unwilling to take upon themselves. Yet this grace, one of the final stages of poverty, is an essential spiritual reality which we must be willing to embrace as a gift from God. The grace we tend to avoid at every cost—and fear with all our hearts—is disgrace! Next to death itself, we cannot bear the loss of our reputation, of our good name.

For those who live north of the sun-and-surf line, autumn arrives each year with the reminder that death comes to all of us quicker than we would like to believe. Autumn awakens us to the fact that harsh winter is close at hand. She who is so rich in harvest gifts and sunset colors calls us to leave behind all illusion. Most of us desire to be wrapped warmly in illusion, safe from our fears about dying. And as our culture becomes less and less religious, a belief in immortality becomes more and more tenuous. We live with only a faint hope of personal immortality, and so the thought of death can be unbearable.

Rollo May wrote of this state:

> Consequently, the awareness of death is widely repressed
> in our day. But none of us can fail to be aware at the

same time of the tremendous preoccupation with sex: in our humor, our drama, and our economic life, even down to the commercials on television. An obsession drains off anxiety from some other area and prevents the person from having to confront something distasteful. What would we have to see if we could cut through our obsession about sex? That we must die. The clamor of sex about us drowns out the ever-waiting presence of death.

Avoidance of thoughts about dying is born from the lack of a profound belief in a personal immortality. And our obsession with our reputation is born of a lack of trust in what accompanies immortality: divine justice. For those who live only for this world, what this world thinks of them is extremely important. To be respectable is an addiction more deadly than heroin. Average middle class people rely on the opinions of others as a yardstick for behavior, saying—if only under their breaths—"What will the neighbors think?" While that is a favorite expression among Irish families, we are all sons and daughters of immigrants, all of whom were held in low esteem, considered to be stupid or backward. Although Irish, Polish or German immigrants would not likely have heard of Publius Syrus, who lived in the first century B.C., they would have all agreed with his wisdom: "A good reputation is more valuable than money." They also believed, even if they had not read the Bible, the saying from Ecclesiastes: "A good name is better than precious ointment" (Eccl. 7: 1). Most of us would also nod in agreement at these statements.

A reputation is an invisible halo of light and admiration with which we encircle the famous, the popular and the talented. But if for some reason they should lose their reputations, the lights go out and the halo drops around their necks. A darkened halo becomes a hangman's noose! You and I fear a fallen halo even if ours is only dimly lit. We greatly fear the loss of our good name; some of us fear it even more than death. Bodily death can be respectable, but it takes a poet or painter to adequately represent the terror of a person disgraced by the exposure of some hidden failing or scandalous deed or by being associated closely with someone who has been shamed. The poet-playwright William Shakespeare movingly described such a disgrace in his play *Othello*. In response to Iago's question, "Are you hurt?" Cassio says, "Reputation, reputation, reputation! Oh! I have lost my reputation. I have lost the immortal part of myself, and what remains is bestial."

Like Cassio, we are mortally wounded by disgrace. We can suffer a deep and life-long wound for a single mistake in the midstream of a good life, for a human weakness exposed. And because we are a tribal people, the loss of reputation brings shame not only to oneself but to one's family, close friends and associates. No one is an island, and just as we share in the glory of others and are suntanned by their success, so we are also singed by the shame of their disgrace. An unmarried daughter who is pregnant, a member of the family who is a drunk, a son arrested for using drugs, a close friend who is revealed as a homosexual, a divorce—any such disgrace can cause a family to move in among the "socially deceased." So we worry about our personal or corporate reputation and what our family or neighbors think of us. And since we can be shamed just by association, our anxiety level is great. That anxiety level is further heightened by the fact that disgrace can come even if we are falsely accused.

Many have been proven guilty of crimes that they never committed! Though the law states that we are innocent until proven guilty, just an allegation can leave an indelible mark on one's reputation. What if you were charged with rape or adultery, that accusation tattooed on people's minds by television and made photo-clear on the front page of the newspaper? Even if the court proved you innocent, in the courtrooms of countless kitchens and among the jurors of ten o'clock coffee breaks, you might stand convicted for life.

"Learn of me," Jesus says, "for I am meek and humble of heart" (Mt. 11: 29). That is indeed a central lesson for those who travel the high road of the spiritual quest, for those who seek to be holy. Humility is the full acceptance of oneself, accepting the gifts and weaknesses of who one is. Christlike humility does not seek fame, praise or the halos given out by this world.

It only seeks the love of God—which is, thank goodness, unconditional love. The awareness of being loved so totally is the energizing agent of true humility. As long as I can be ashamed of myself or a companion, I know that I have not yet reached true humility. Such humility is far from easy, yet it is a degree of humility that we can learn from our great teacher and spiritual guide, Jesus. "Learn from me," he says. "Learn from the disgrace of my life that was my **real grace**. I ate and drank with enjoyment, and people said, 'Here is a glutton and a drunkard, a friend of tax collectors and sinners!' (Lk. 7: 34). Though innocent, I was accused by liars and judged guilty. I was led in shame through the streets, mocked, exposed to ridicule and subjected to a disgraceful execution. Yes, learn to accept disgrace willingly, accept the whole of the human condition."

In the thirteenth chapter of the ancient holy book of China, the *Tao Te Ching*, it says:

> Accept disgrace willingly. Accept misfortune as the human condition. What do you mean by 'accept disgrace willingly?' Accept being unimportant. Do not be concerned with loss or gain. This is called accepting disgrace willingly...Surrender yourself humbly; then you can be trusted to care for all things. Love the world as your own self; then you can truly care for all things.

Humility is accepting the human condition. That acceptance acknowledges that in your family closet and mine there are skeletons that may hold the power to disgrace or cause embarrassment. Like Jesus, you and I can be accused of sins or crimes we have not committed. Or at one time in our lives we may have done something that would disgrace us if it were made public. We have no obligation to publicize such a failure, but we should be ready if God gives us the grace of disgrace. "Learn of me," says Jesus. That is not a call to philosophical reflection but an invitation to wholeness by embracing nothingness.

A halo is a golden zero that encircles your head. As long as we refuse to let it become a true zero, we will never earn a saintly halo but only a secular halo of success. Disgrace is a grace by which we are stripped of our good name, more precious to us than money. To accept disgrace willingly is to be open to a divine visitation whose purpose is to empty us of our false, self-important identity which stands in the way of realizing who we really are. To become a zero, a nothing, is to accept being unimportant, as the *Tao* said. To become a zero does not mean nonexistence but rather simply being just as we are. As Jesus knew so well, it is surrendering to another set of values, to divine judgment rather than a social or religious judgment.

The National Enquirer is hardly "good news," yet its popularity stems from our greedy hunger to hear "bad news" about others, especially those to whom we have given halos of fame. Jesus proclaimed the Good News that failure, weakness and disgrace can be God's womb for true greatness. We have only to look at how our Teacher willingly embraced disgrace and lived out the way of the cross because it was the way of heaven. Naturally, this is madness when viewed from our success-oriented value system. "Learn of me," says the Teacher. "Learn how I placed my hope and trust not in my reputation, not in the good and holy things that I did, not in the miracles and wonders that I performed. No, my hope was in God alone. My humility sprang from the belief that I was loved simply for being who I was." We know that his hope was not in vain.

As you ponder how you might respond if you were falsely accused or if some embarrassing human failing were exposed, place your hope and trust in God and in those who truly love you. Like Jesus' mother, his women friends and his close disciple John, who stood tall and clear beside the cross in his hour of shame, anyone who truly loves you will stand beside you regardless of the risk to their reputations. To one on the High Road, "what the neighbors think" is not important.

If the grace of disgrace should be our gift from God, let's see in it an opportunity to be free of our addiction to human approval and social acceptance. For some people, by God's choice, humiliation is the door to true humility. If we have learned from our Teacher, then that doorway is not entered with dread. If we have prepared ourselves by a daily acceptance of being unimportant, we will be sure in the knowledge that we are greatly loved, even if we are nailed in disgrace. To become a zero is to have the best halo possible. Then, though we may own a Cadillac, sleep on silk sheets and eat caviar for breakfast, we are truly living in poverty. However, if we are unable to accept disgrace with grace, then even if we go barefoot, begging for food from door to door, we have never truly embraced "Lady Poverty." It is said that the door to heaven is low and narrow, but I suspect that it is round and small—like a zero!

Nothing Without Sacrifice

In his novel, *The Strange Life of Ivan Osokin*, P.D. Ouspensky tells the tale of a young man who was so depressed that he was contemplating suicide. It seems that at every crossroads he had taken the wrong turn, and now he was experiencing life as a complete waste. He went to an old wise man, a magician and sorcerer, and pleaded with him to perform some magic. The young man thought that if he had another chance he could do better. So he asked the magician to send him back to the time of his birth so that he could relive his life. The sorcerer refused, telling him that no magic would make it possible for him to change. The young man, however, pleaded with the sage until he granted his wish. So he was returned to begin life once again. Nevertheless, even though he knew what would happen to him at each turn of his life, he was unable to prevent the same mistakes from happening again. After living his life a second time, he once again came to the old sorcerer. Only this time he was even more depressed than before because his failure at life was now doubled!

> The magician said to him, "My son, nothing can be acquired without sacrifice. This is the thing you do not understand, and until you understand it, nothing can be done. Had I wanted to give you, without sacrifice on your part, everything you might wish, I could not have

done it. A man can only be given what he can use; and he can use only that for which he has sacrificed something...So if a man wants to get new powers or knowledge, he must sacrifice other things important to him at the moment. Moreover, he can only get as much as he has given up for it.''

The young man asked, ''Are there no other ways?''

And the magician replied, ''You mean ways in which no sacrifice is necessary? No, there are no other such ways, and you do not understand what you are asking. You cannot have results without causes. By your sacrifice you create causes.''

''By your sacrifice you create causes.'' With these words Ouspensky's sorcerer gave to the young man and to us the magical formula for love, holiness and success. If you want to become holy, if you want to achieve greatness in any field, if you want to have a happy marriage or a rewarding life, then remember the wisdom of the magician and ask yourself: ''What important thing at this moment am I willing to sacrifice in order to achieve what I greatly desire?''

If you want your marriage to be different from all the others that have crashed upon the rocks, then you will have to sacrifice. If you wish to experience the rare gift of friendship, a relationship of depth and intimacy, then you will have to sacrifice. If you wish to develop your inner life so that it is a source of peace and strength—if you wish to pray daily, to meditate regularly—then you will have to sacrifice. If you wish to have a happy and full life, finding enjoyment in what you do and who you are, then you will have to sacrifice. If you wish to follow your dream, to give flesh to your truest desire, then you will have to sacrifice. Like the young man in the story, we plead, ''Isn't there some other way?'' The answer comes back from all four corners of the cosmos: ''No, my friend, there are no other ways. And if you ask the question, you do not understand what you are asking, and you do not understand how the universe works!''

In a society where discomfort is avoided at every opportunity, sacrifice is a dirty word. In such a comfort culture people usually attempt to escape from any demands of self-sacrifice through a variety of compromises. Self-denial in such a society is viewed as nonproductive to self-realization. As a result, few persons ask themselves or others to make sacrifices. Yet without sacrifice as a constant element in our lives, we cannot be happy or holy. Sacrifice is an essential part of the life process; it is a universal spiritual activity. I am not aware of a religion which does not have some ritual of sacrifice. This most ancient and ageless form of prayer is also the most cosmic.

The word sacrifice comes from two Latin words, *sacra*, meaning "holy" and *facio*, meaning "to make." Hence all sacrifice is "to make holy." The intent of a religious ritual of sacrifice is to make something or someone holy. Throughout history sacrifice has been **the** way to become holy. Rituals have involved the offering up of animals, food and even human life in order to acquire favors from the gods, to keep them happy or to amend some action that caused guilt or remorse. In the early times of our Judeo-Christian tradition the king or the head of the family offered the sacrifice. Patriarchs like Abraham and Noah presided over sacrifices, but eventually the ritual was restricted to priests.

Today we often view such "primitive" religious behavior with a smile, considering ourselves to be "beyond" such childlike expressions. Themes of celebration, rejoicing and new life have replaced—or at least overlaid—the idea of sacrifice in our worship and theology. The concept of sacrifice may have to be rediscovered at a deeper level even by theologians—as well as by those who seek a mystical communion with the Divine Mystery. We will have to learn to see beyond the external oblation of sheep or wheat to the mystical meaning of sacrifice. What if the real original intent of this surrendering was not fear but communion? What if sacrifice is a much more essential part of human existence than just an act of expiation? If so, then the words of the old magician in Ouspensky's story would have a real impact on anyone walking a spiritual pathway.

Even a passing glance at the great religions of the world reveals a profound reverence for the act of sacrifice. In the Hindu scriptures of India there are countless quotes about sacrifice which are summed up well in these lines from the *Bhagavad Gita*: "Whatever you do, whatever you eat, whatever your offering, whatever your alms or penance, do it all as a sacrifice to Me." This notion of worship is not limited solely to prayer. It is very much involved in the **action** of sacrifice, during which duality is transcended and the worshiper becomes one with God. Among the American Plains Indians the notion of sacrifice was equally essential. In the Sun Dance, suffering was embraced so that life could go on. Only in this essential religious action of sacrifice was final freedom to be found and laughter returned to the earth. If we find such a global reverence for ritual sacrifice, why didn't Jesus also require it?

Jesus repeated the criticism of sacrifice voiced by the prophets of Israel. He echoed the words of Hosea: "It is love that I desire, not sacrifice, and knowledge of God rather than holocausts" (Hos. 6: 6). Such expressions could easily lead us to believe that Jesus and the prophets were opposed to the long tradition of ritual sacrifice in Judaism, going back to Abraham and Cain and Abel. They were, rather, opposed to the lack of an inner spirit of sacrifice that made external rituals hollow of holiness and therefore roadblocks to those on the Way. If we look closely at Jesus' other words, we see that he actually requires of those who want to follow him a sacrifice of **everything**: possessions, home, family and even their very selves! Jesus speaks to the deeper implications of sacrifice when he says, "Unless the grain of wheat falls to the earth and dies, it remains just a grain of wheat. But if it dies, it produces much fruit" (Jn. 12: 24).

Every sacrifice is a death, a dying to self. In the mystical tradition of Islam, the prophet Mohammed was said to have given this concise instruction: "Die before you die." Again, it is the call to make oneself the victim of a sacrifice for the sake of communion with the One. The unreal self needs to die so that a more authentic self might appear. We hear it prayed in Psalm 39: "You do not ask for sacrifice and offerings; instead, here am I." Such sacrifice is the way, the law of love. And those who fail to know the law of love will fail to learn how to truly love others, to *become* love. If you desire a relationship with another person that has depth and quality, then you must be willing to give up (sacrifice) time, petty interests, money, your personal vantage point and a host of other things that are important to you at the time. Daily we offer sacrifice whenever we say "no" to ourselves so that we can say "yes" to another. That "no" must be freely and willingly offered if the sacrifice is to be pure and powerful. The author of Ephesians tells us, "Follow the way of love, even as Christ loved you. He gave himself for us as an offering to God, a gift of pleasing fragrance" (Eph. 5: 2). The way of love, then, involves sacrificing ourselves. But how?

Whenever we choose not to do what we want because of a love for others, that is sacrifice. Whenever we refuse to allow an unkind thought about another to take up residence in our minds, that is sacrifice. Whenever we refuse to speak a word that will bring unnecessary pain to another, then we are acting as a priest—we are offering sacrifice.

All sacrifice by its very nature involves suffering. But suffering, like danger, has the power to release vast amounts of energy. That energy has qualities of both physical vitality and of light. Shamans, mystics, prophets and holy ones of the past understood the universe to be nourished by such unseen but real energies of light. That awareness gave sacrifice a tribal, national, global and even cosmic dimension. Besides effecting a release of energy, sacrifice also has the power to create a bridge, a link, between the "victim" of the sacrifice and others, between the "victim" and God. The aim of the inner journey in the Buddhist view of spiritual sacrifice is giving up the false individual self to become part of the Whole. Self-sacrifice leads to a reunion with nature, society and the Divine. Self-oblation is the act of reconciliation, and therefore redemption.

Jesus invited his followers to "remember" his sacrifice: "Do this in memory of me" (Lk. 22:19). By his personal sacrifice he released infinite amounts of "light" energy to heal a broken and divided world. By his death and total surrender, he entered into a complete and cosmic unity with the Father. Sacrifice creates a bond of union between the giver of the gift and the receiver that cannot be repeated too often. In this mysterious principle of unity giving a gift creates a deeper and more intimate connection than receiving one. Understanding this principle helps us understand our need to give to God. In Abraham's readiness to sacrifice his only son, his beloved Isaac, and Jesus' willingness to give himself in sacrifice to the Father, we have two models of that highest desire to achieve total intimacy with God.

To embrace pain intentionally might be viewed as masochistic, a sickness in which a person finds pleasure in self-inflicted pain. But sacrifice is sought not for the "pleasure" of pain but for the possession of love. A person freely suffers the loss of something valuable for the sake of something more valuable. Such sacrificial suffering is creative and life-giving. Bearing the pain of a headache without taking any medicine or without stopping to rest and understand the tension that has created the pain is not creative suffering, even if it is done for the love of God. On the other hand, we can sacrifice creatively by freely choosing to set aside time daily to read from books that will add to our understanding of life, prayer or God. We might also rise from sleep a half hour earlier to have time to meditate, to pray privately, before our day begins. It would be wholesome sacrifice to refuse to take part in any action which discriminates against another or promotes injustice. To act on our convictions at the cost of losing the good opinions of others is positive sacrifice that pleases God and is pure worship. We all feel the magnetic pull of consumerism, the hypnotic call to "buy, buy, buy." Consumerism works against sacrifice because it proposes self-indulgence instead of self-denial. As a small part of a greater and poorer world, we Americans will have to make changes in our lifestyles in the coming years. The virtue of self-sacrifice can become truly a radical and revolutionary lifestyle at the dawning of a new millennium.

If you are still reading this reflection, then you have made a sacrifice. In the first place, you have chosen to do this instead of something else. The very reading of this attempt to explore the meaning of sacrifice has been for you a sacrifice—and an act of worship and prayer. It is also a sign that you desire to be more than ordinary; to be more than an ordinary wife, husband, teacher, single parent, student, minister, nun, priest or spiritual seeker. If we seek greatness (and we should, so that the mystery of God will shine out from us in luminous splendor), then we must be willing to make the sacrifices required to achieve a largeness of being. The real "stars" in sports, theater, the arts, literature, politics or spirituality all know this law of sacrifice. They have become what they are because of their willingness to make sacrifices. For those who desire to become what God has willed them to be—to become saints—the pathway is paved with a willingness to live a radical and redeeming lifestyle. Such a desire, however, has a cost, as the following story from the East shows:

> Once there was a man who wanted to have a lion tattooed on his back. He went to the tattoo shop and told the owner of his wish. But as soon as he felt the first few pricks of the tattoo needle, he began to groan, "You're killing me. What part of the lion are you marking?"
>
> "I'm just doing the tail now," said the artist.
>
> "Then let's leave out the tail," said the man. Once more the artist started, but soon the man again complained of the pain, "What part of the lion are you doing now?"
>
> "The lion's ear," said the tattooist.
>
> "Then let's leave off the ear," gasped the man. So the tattooist began again, only to hear, "What are you doing now?"
>
> "The lion's stomach," the artist wearily replied.
>
> "Let's leave off the stomach," said the man. "I don't want a lion with a stomach."
>
> At that the tattoo artist said, "A lion without a tail, ears and stomach is no lion! Perhaps you would rather have an ant's image on your back instead!"

If we desire to become "living" images of God, then we will have to be open to lives of sacrifice while that sacred image is tattooed upon us. However, if we reject sacrifice and its accompanying pain, we will have to be content with a life that falls far short of the grand design that God has dreamed for us. Let us conclude this reflection with a prayer that we can sacrifice in new and creative ways, that we can become, as St. Paul said, "living sacrifices, holy and acceptable to God" (Rom. 12: 1).

Light a Candle

One day as Jesus was praying, one of his disciples said to him, "Lord, teach us to pray." And Jesus said to them, "When you want to pray, light a candle." Peter turned to his brother Andrew and said, "Light a what? What's a candle?" Andrew shrugged his shoulders in a gesture of confusion. Again, Jesus said, "Amen, amen, I say to you, when you want to pray, light a candle." His disciples, however, did not understand what Jesus was saying.

This "rewritten" Gospel story about lighting a candle when you want to pray is not a spiritual riddle or parable. Quite simply, the disciples would not have known about candles, which were first made only two thousand years ago. This invention of portable light would thus have been foreign to the simple fishermen of backwoods Galilee. As we know from Gospel stories, the means of illumination for them was what it had been for thousands of years: oil lamps. We who live in the electric age know about candles, even though they are used primarily for decoration. They appear inside jack-o'-lanterns, grace our festive Thanksgiving Day tables and stand in purple vigil around Advent wreaths. Candles take turns announcing the joy of Hanukkah, and their lights dance in our windows at Christmas time.

Candles are also emergency lights for storms and power

failures. And, of course, they are a traditional part of worship services in our churches. Their relationship to prayer, however, is often only a background decoration. So, even for us the words of Jesus about lighting a candle to pray can seem puzzling. With Peter we too can respond to those imaginary words of Jesus by asking, "Light a what?" To help us understand Jesus' advice in the story, we might look more closely at our use of candles in church and at other times.

We use candlelight for worship as a relic of the days when it had a practical purpose. Over the centuries it has come to be identified with the "holy." Those of the Catholic tradition have been unconsciously conditioned to associate a lighted candle with the presence of the Divine Mystery since a vigil light burns before the tabernacle day and night. The burning candle also says, "God is here" on the altar at times of worship. Candles also have special significance on feast days and during sacred seasons. Christmas, which carries the theme of light in the darkness, uses the candle's flaming symbol to signify the dawning of a new age. Christianity's other great feast, Easter, is graced by the tall, majestic paschal candle, which symbolizes the new life of the Resurrection. Candles flicker before icons and shrines as signs of reverence. People with special petitions light candles as prayer offerings and as signs that their prayers are aflame before God long after they have left church.

We also use candles for less specifically religious occasions. Candlelight implies love, romance and affection. At romantic times we usually prefer candles to bright electric lights. They carry a mood of intimacy suggested by their use next to tabernacles and in small, darkened chapels and crypts. In addition, dinner parties, weddings and birthdays come alive with the flicker of candlelight.

Why do these small, wax-wrapped wicks with their tiny flames call us to romance, celebration and prayerfulness? Whenever you light a candle, you light a memory. It may not necessarily even be one of *your* memories but rather one of *ours*. We all possess personal memories, but we also have communal memories which echo back to the beginnings of the human family.

Alive and well, even though buried deeply inside of us, are these ancient memories, these primitive codes and echoes. They include memories of primal fears and joys, of victories and defeats. Among them, contained within the core of each of these old, old memories, is the memory of God. Whenever we are touched by wonder, by a sense of awe, an old memory is awakened and prayer begins! When you touch a match to a candle, you "light up" such a memory, even if you are not conscious of igniting such primitive recall.

Darkness and death are banished by fire and light. To our cave-dwelling great-grandparents light was a miracle as wondrous as walking on water. Fire was for them either a gift from the gods or a prize stolen from the hearth of the holy ones. Regardless, firelight was a divine possession and therefore a form of holy communion. Even with all our sophistication, the child within delights at the wonder-full and sacred sight of fire!

So when you light a candle, you begin to pray—even if you never say a word or mention God's name. Dinners by candlelight are innate prayer, and birthday cakes when they shimmer with candle fire are truly worship. When friends sit together, sharing a glass of wine within the sacred circle of candlelight, there is a Presence that makes their conversation prayerful poetry. In these and other times we can draw a direct and mystical line of association between the sanctuary candle that burns both day and night before the tabernacle and the candles burning softly in any joyful or romantic setting. They are all signs proclaiming that **God is with us**. Since prayer means being in the presence of God, we truly pray whenever we sense the Mystery. It is certainly possible to pray and not be aware of the divine presence or even that we are praying. In fact, one of the greatest surprises that will be reserved for us in heaven is the knowledge of how often we were "at prayer" but didn't know it! Yet even if we are not aware of the prayerful power inherent in candles, they help make us aware of the Divine Mystery.

Candles, which give solace and hope in the dark and cold of winter, are also sacraments of one of the oldest mysteries: fire. To light a candle is to kindle a tiny fire. Along with earth, air

and water, fire has been one of the great symbols of God. In the First Testament it is often a living sign of God's presence. Moses was told that the ground around the burning bush was "holy" and that he was to take off his shoes in reverence. A pillar of fire led the Hebrews on their Exodus and surrounded Mt. Sinai. "For the Lord, your God," the book of Deuteronomy tells us, "is a consuming fire" (Dt. 4: 24). And in the temple of Jerusalem, the fire on the altar of the whole burnt offerings was to burn perpetually as a symbol of the abiding presence of Yahweh. Jesus too spoke of his mission in terms of fire: "I have come to bring **fire** on the earth and desire that it be kindled" (Lk. 12: 49).

It is difficult today to light a fire. Laws forbid the burning of trash and autumn leaves. Some day people may grow up and never know firsthand the experience of fire. Perhaps because on some level we are aware that we are losing touch with that primal sacred element of fire, fireplaces and wood-burning stoves have had a resurgence in popularity. For the majority of us, however, fire as a companion in our everyday lives is only a memory—but what a memory! Is it the thrill of racing red fire engines that can make children want to follow the sirens, or is it the promise of fire? Perhaps we are roused by fire because it reminds us of the sun, the star which makes all life on our planet possible. Perhaps fire further reminds us of the flaming solar wombs from which we and all creation have come. You and I, like the rest of the stuff of this planet, are stardust from the burned-out fires of dead stars. Indeed, how old, how truly old, might the **memory** be?

If you are fortunate enough to be able to spend time in front of a crackling fire in a fireplace in the winter, reflect on these words. Meditate on the magic of the fire to attract us, its capacity to relax and heal us and to put us into a romantic mood. Since we believe that God is love, that magic should not surprise or shock us. The smell of the smoke and the ritual of feeding the fire can all become times of prayer, even if we never say "Let us pray" or conclude with "Amen."

The power of candles or fire to set a romantic mood can awaken us to another unexplored possibility. What if romance is God's non-religious sanctuary. It would certainly make sense to heighten such times with the use of candlelight. However, what can we do if we have a meal or visit with a friend and no candle is provided? Perhaps we can allow the mystical marvel that happened to Moses to be our experience as well. While tending his sheep, a common bush became aflame with fire. We can cause a bush, a table, the pictures in a room or whatever is at hand to "light up." The salt and pepper shakers, the ketchup bottle and the plastic napkin holder can all burst into flames that burn but do not consume. For those with contemplative eyes, every bush or every table can be aflame with the presence of God.

If candles and fires are truly to lead us into prayer, we will have to respect them and find conscious ways to use them. We can begin right at the beginning: with the lighting of the candle. As practical Americans we tend to treat this act as a necessity instead of a meaningful ritual. A flick of the match and the candle is "turned on." Perhaps it is our frequent contact with electric light switches that has dulled us to the ritual of lighting candles. Birthday cakes, dinner parties, wedding receptions— even candles lit in worship—are usually "turned on" without graceful ceremony or conscious thought. If we are conscious of the "memories" and of the Mystery, would it not be natural to have a spoken or silent moment of ritual whenever we light candles?

In the Jewish Shabbat meal which is celebrated each Friday in the homes of devout Jews, the mother of the family lights the table candles with a beautiful prayer:

> Come, let us welcome the Sabbath. May its radiance illumine our hearts as we kindle these candles. Light is the symbol of the divine. Light is the symbol of the divine in us. Light is the symbol of the divine law. Therefore, in the spirit of our ancient tradition that hallows and unites Israel in all lands and all ages, do we now kindle the Sabbath lights *(candles are lit)*. May our home be consecrated, O God, by thy light. May it shine upon us all in blessing as the light of love and truth, the light of peace and goodwill.

We can compose our own ritual, even if it contains only a word or two. We could simply but slowly make the sign of the cross with the burning match before we blow it out. We could also do nothing, simply looking with silent wonder at the flame, allowing it to bless our eyes and our hearts with the marvel of God's luminous presence. In the age of microwave ovens and neon lights, candles and fires give us an opportunity to remember, to touch again, those most ancient memories that lie sleeping in our DNA codes. To use them when we pray alone can add a dimension of communion to our prayer that may surprise us. To use them at special meals can transform our family kitchen table into an altar-shrine. To look upon any place where they burn as holy ground will make us more reverent, even if we are wearing our shoes.

Candles and fires are not only the stuff of memories, they are also prophets—visionaries of what is to come. At the close of one millennium and the dawning of a new one, evangelical prophets of doom are painting grim images of our little planet's demise by fire. However, if fire is the human family's oldest symbol of the Eternal Presence, if it is a sign of romance and of the blazing love of God, then perhaps for our world to end in fire might be for it to end in love. As the American poet Robert Frost said,

> Some say the world will end in fire,
> some say in ice.
> From what I've tasted of desire
> I hold with those who favor fire.

Unplug

One of the marvelous gifts of technology is the telephone. We soon discovered, however, that in the gift is also hidden a curse. What a great benefit to be able to speak to someone far away at any time we wish. On the other hand, we are cursed that at any time, day or night, the telephone can intrude upon whatever we are doing. The telephone veritably demands our attention. Alas, the gift of being able to talk with others at any hour has almost become the curse of *having* to talk with others at any hour!

However, modern technology has also provided us with a cure for the curse. In so doing it has given us a contemporary symbol for how to live in a manner that leads to wholeness and holiness. This gift-cure of technology is the "unplugable" telephone! Now, when we don't care to have others interrupt what we are doing, we can simply unplug our servant, the telephone, and so keep it from becoming a master.

The "unplugable" telephone is a new symbol of freedom. It also speaks of the need to unplug other aspects of modern technological living at certain times. The numerous electrical machines that are part of our daily lives are mechanical servants which perform tasks once done by human servants or by ourselves. Understandably, we hesitate to pull the plug on mechanical servants for we fear that we will be abandoned. Yet just the opposite can be true. When we unplug any modern machine, another servant is suddenly free to appear.

Every time we unplug a machine that does a job, we are forced to find another way of doing that work. Usually we fall back on a pre-technological way to perform the same task. As a result of its age, it is usually slower and more human, more creative and re-creative, and almost always more quiet. When I unplug my electric typewriter, I pick up a pen and begin to create the mysterious signs and symbols called letters which, unlike a printing machine, reveal much of my personality by the way I make them. When I unplug my television set, a servant appears with a bow and says, "Why not entertain yourself? Why not go outside and play ball instead of watching others play? Why not go and do something adventuresome instead of watching a synthetic adventure?"

Being "unplugged," then, is a fitting image for the revolution we need at the dawning of the twenty-first century. It can be a way to find freedom and "soul" in our hectic lives. Machines do not have souls, but our souls need food, exercise and care— all requirements for human wellness. Technology, on the other hand, has the power to be of great assistance and to raise the quality of our lives. Of course, it has the power to dehumanize as well!

Besides occasionally unplugging the telephone or television, we must also muster the courage to "unplug" ourselves from our workplace and even to be free at times from our vocations or avocations. When we "unplug" from our usual occupations, we cut off the flow of corporate current that surges through us even when we are miles away from the work itself. That powerful current flows through us at unconscious levels and is a prime cause of weariness. Being constantly "on the job" prevents us from savoring our souls. Those who never "unplug" inevitably lack soul and spirit. St. Paul in his letter to the Romans tells us, "You are not in the flesh; you are in the spirit, since the Spirit of God dwells in you" (Rom. 8: 9). As Jesus warned, we can easily lose touch with our spirit by an excessive concern about winning the rewards of the world.

Do not misunderstand. This chapter is not condemning technology or urging that you return to primitive log cabin living. The evil enters only when we are constantly "plugged in." Revolutions are begun for the liberation of the oppressed. So many people in modern Western society have allowed their technological servants to enslave them that we could use this slogan for a new revolution: "Rise Up, Be Free and Unplug Yourselves!" We all need to be released from the constant demands and slave-like patterns of our contemporary lives if we are to increase the richness of our souls. We need times, even whole days, of setting aside the normal burdens of daily life so that we can be fully human again. For to be constantly "plugging away" robs us of our souls and makes all of life into a burden.

We need to remember what God told Moses, "Six days you may labor and do all your work; but the seventh day is the Sabbath of your God. No work may be done then, whether by you or...your male or female slave...For remember that you too were once slaves in Egypt and that your God brought you from there with a strong arm" (Dt. 5: 13-15). Jewish people observe the Sabbath by remembering that they were once enslaved but are now free. *Sabbath* literally means "to rest," but another way of saying it is "to unplug."

It is a tradition in Judaism, Islam and Christianity to observe a weekly day in honor of God. Saturday is set aside by Jews, Friday by Moslems and Sunday by Christians. The actual day may not be as important as how it is observed. Perhaps a story may assist us in that understanding:

> After God had created the world and all that was to live upon it and had divided time into seven days, the devil came demanding an equal share of time. God proposed that they divide the week equally, each taking three and one-half days. But the devil instead suggested that they play poker for the possession of the days. Now, God knew that the devil always cheated when he played poker, but God just smiled and asked for a fresh deck of cards.
>
> The devil insisted that the stakes for the first game be the first and last days of the workweek. By means of

an underhanded maneuver the devil won the first game. Gathering up his winnings, he said to himself, "Ah, I can get each week off to a bad start by putting people on the wrong foot. I can instill ruthless competition and other vices on the first day of work, and with the last day I can show them delicious ways to 'let their hair down' after a weary week of labor." As they approached the final game, God had allowed the devil to win six whole days! Only one day remained, and with a river-boat gambler's flourish, God laid out a royal flush on the table and won the seventh day.

The devil walked away from the green-topped card table chuckling to himself, "Great winning odds, six to one! With odds like that I can't help but win the whole world."

As God arose from the table, a circle of angels who had watched the card game shook their heads in dismay. "Why, O God," they said, "did you let that cheating devil win six of the seven days? What can you do with only one day?"

God answered them, "Oh, I've got special plans. I only need one day; that's more than enough!"

An angel spoke up, "Of course, we should have guessed. One full day of prayer and worship will give your children the strength they need to remain faithful to you for the other six."

God smiled. "That wasn't what I had in mind. All I need is one day for them to **enjoy** me! They can savor me when they enjoy leisure, when they rest. I shall tell them to keep it holy. If they can just remember to keep it restful, it will be godlike and holy!"

This parable addresses the question of whether the Lord's Day is intended to be a day of worship or of rest. Isn't the primary prayer of that holy day to be "unplugged"? The Sabbath is a day to remember that we are no longer slaves. Revolutions, if they are to be continuously liberating, demand constant watch-fulness and self-discipline. All too often we allow ourselves to be slowly enslaved by other forms of oppression. Christians, Jews and Moslems—perhaps we have all forgotten the primal purpose of God's Day and so find our lives a burden. Jesus says to us, "Come to me, all you who are weary and find life burdensome, and I will refresh you" (Mt. 11: 28).

Our chains make life burdensome. Some of those chains are electrical cords and all that they symbolize. When we "unplug" from our workday tasks, we can "plug into" another source of energy. This source surges electrically and vitally in the gentle movement of the wind or the soft sound of rain dripping from the roof. Creation is charged with this healing energy, as is quiet inner prayer. In fact, this energy source is always and everywhere available. If we routinely "unplug" ourselves, we will find that it is not difficult to recognize more of who we really are. In becoming fully human, in reconnecting to our souls, we will be able to make love or to celebrate life with more soul and heart and zeal. God's Day is for restoration.

In the Jewish mystic tradition, the world is "resouled" every Sabbath, every seventh day. Those who observe this special day of the week "grow" in soul. The Hebrew word used in Scripture for "rested" (as in "God rested on the seventh day") is *nefesh* which also means "soul."

A tale is told about a king who invited one of his subjects to come and dwell in his royal palace. The subject said, "I have a friend whom I love so dearly that I never allow myself to dwell apart from him. I accept your invitation only if you also invite my friend to come and live in the palace."

This story suggests that the soul refuses to be parted from the body, that body and soul cannot be separated in any activity. True joy can only come when both share fully in any of life's activities. But unless we experience the reality of our souls, how will body and soul ever be intimate friends? We need a day a week, at least, to taste and feel the Spirit of God that dwells within us. We would also do well to set aside a time each day for a conscious reunion of body and soul. When such reunions happen frequently, we will know, like the subject in the story about the king, which invitations to accept and which ones to turn down. Then our whole selves will be present in everything we do.

The Seventh Day is "soul" day. Honoring it is essential if

we are to "resoul" the world as well as the work of our hands. Churches, synagogues and all places of prayer where we honor the Sabbath might more correctly be named "Rest Rooms!" They should be places where we can "unplug" ourselves and as many of our machine-servants as possible, places where we can "plug into" that divine energy source which electrifies all creation. If we can truly honor that one day a week, we will find refreshment and "resoulment." Then, if we apply the self-discipline necessary to be "unplugged" a part of each day, we will find it much easier to live and love with all our hearts and souls.

It is sad that for all these centuries we have failed to find the surprise gift that God gave to the children of the earth. This treasure came wrapped up as a law, but inside was the most enjoyable and healing gift that any human heart could imagine. Unfortunately, having not found the gift, we have for centuries been caught up in the wrapping. We thought the purpose of the day was prayer when, for God, walking away from his poker table, it was play.

Won Ton Communion

This chapter begins with soup! Here is an old German story about poor little Suppenkasper:

> Once there was a little German boy who resolutely refused to eat his soup. He was a stubborn little lad, and because of his refusal he slowly wasted away. When Suppenkasper died, he was buried with his soup bowl on his cemetery headstone.

This short and sad story is really a parable about ourselves. To understand its implications we need to recall that Christianity is the only truly materialistic religion (at the same time acknowledging Christianity's roots in Judaism). Among the great religions of the world, Christianity uniquely asserts the **total** goodness and glory of the physical universe. She reminds us continuously and in countless ways what God said at the close of each day of creation: "Ummm, that's good!"

Hinduism and Buddhism, for example, are ambivalent about the goodness of the created world. They strive to find ways to rise above it to the "spiritual" realm. They proclaim a theology of transcending the flesh instead of loving it intensely. Reformed Christianity and certain groups within Catholicism tend to join with their brothers and sisters of the East and proclaim a necessity to "rise above," to transcend, our bodies and our passions. Yet at its core Christianity espouses a love and ongoing communion with the material world, now glorified in the Resurrection.

Jesus gave his little community an earthly sacrament in the gift of his body and blood. The supper meal of the Eucharist celebrates the union of Jesus with humanity and the earth as it rejoices in the union of God with the universe. This union is one of love and intimate communion with creation. The supper meal of Christ's body and blood calls for a religion that we are still waiting to see! It is a religion that daily celebrates the marriage of heaven and earth—not a token union, but a real marriage. Poor little Suppenkasper refused his soup. It seems that we do the same to our invitation to the wedding of heaven and earth.

For 550 million years (give or take a few million), earth and heaven have had an on-again off-again romance. While all that was created has been called "good" theologically, it has usually been "good" with reservations. A conditional clause is inevitably inserted: "Yes, creation is good **if**...yes, good and holy, **but**... ." Why has the full marriage been delayed? It's all the "ifs" and "buts" that have prevented the appearance of a religion of the marriage of heaven and earth.

Alan Watts said that we have never been able to say what every true lover says, "I love you with ALL my heart." As a result of that inability, we Christians who possess the rare possibility of a truly materialistic religion continue to live with the world like an erratic lover.

The awesome words of Jesus, "This is my body..." challenge us to love that body, which is a cosmic body, a body that includes the whole universe. Those simple but profound words, "This is my body," have divided Christians into two basic groups. There are those who believe that it is exactly as he said, the full reality of the gift of himself. Others believe that it is only a token, a pious—though beautiful—symbol. The verb "is" is important, for the body we dine upon is not that of the historic Jesus but the living, risen and glorious body, the cosmic Body of Christ. The mystery of the Body of Christ is that the gift of Our Lord is not simply flesh and blood but the whole person of

Christ. Perhaps our failure to understand and be fully nourished by the sacred meal of the Eucharist is because, like poor little Suppenkasper, we do not eat our soup!

Every great dinner begins with soup, that unsurpassed appetite stimulant. Each time we Christians gather to celebrate the Lord's Supper, that experience should also begin with a sacred soup course! If we are to be fully nourished in Holy Communion with the Cosmic Body of Christ, there is no better way to begin that meal than with *won ton* communion!

If you enjoy Chinese food, then you are probably familiar with won tons. They are light, fluffy pastry creations filled with pork, chicken, shrimp or crab meat and placed in a wonderful soup. In Chinese *won* means "cloud" and *ton* means "to swallow." They do resemble the high, fluffy white clouds that drift across the summer sky. Their Chinese creator was a gourmet genius to name them won tons, for eating them is like swallowing a cloud. As they slip down the throat, we find that while they do not have a silver lining, they are filled with mouthwatering crab meat or pork!

Won tons are not only like clouds in their outward appearance, but also, like clouds, they can surprise us with the mystery contained within them. In the case of sky clouds, the mystery within is water, batches of sky fog. Clouds, like communion, are complicated in their utter simplicity. When the rays of the sun strike water surfaces on the earth, some of the water evaporates. It is then absorbed by the air in the form of water vapor. Air can contain only so much water until it reaches its maximum capacity at a given temperature. The higher the temperature, the greater the capacity to contain moisture. As the temperature of the air begins to cool, some of the water vapor begins to condense, and presto! We have clouds! Won tons and clouds hide within themselves a source of nourishment, and that brings us full circle back to the Body of Christ, Holy Communion! (Recall that you were encouraged to dine upon sacred soup, a Won Ton Communion, prior to the holy main course.)

Won Ton Communion is communion not so much with the Body of Christ as with the Body of God. In the First Testament, the cloud is perhaps the primary way in which Yahweh appears. It was as a cloud that Yahweh led the Israelites on their forty-year journey through the desert. As a cloud, God descended upon Mt. Sinai for the earth's most famous summit conference to offer a covenant marriage between heaven and earth. In the Second Testament, God overshadowed the mountain of the Transfiguration of Jesus and said, "This is my beloved son" (Mk. 9:7). And...

"Well, yes," you may say as you read this, "but aren't those only symbolic images? God didn't actually come as a cloud. God created the clouds, the sun and the moon; they are creations of God, but you can't say that God came as a cloud!" Well, it all depends on how you understand creation. Perhaps God created the world out of nothing or, like a sculptor, produced everything out of elements that were entirely outside the divine being. Then again, creation may be a more intimate expression of God's being. In the notion of *kenosis*, a Greek word which means "outpouring," God is constantly pouring forth creation from within, much as a mother brings forth a child from within her own body. *Kenosis*, as an outpouring of self, is what Jesus did at the Last Supper. "This is my body, given in love for you" (Lk. 22:19).

Won Ton Communion is a necessary preparation, an essential appetizer, because through it we engage in the act of swallowing—being in communion with—God. As a prayerful mini-sacrament it opens to us the possibility of daily communion without having to go to church (very much Jesus' state of being throughout his life). It also is a marvelous contemplative preparation for receiving Holy Communion with the mystical and cosmic Body of Christ. And just how does one experience Won Ton Communion? Well, let's begin with the clouds.

Instead of simply looking at clouds, pick out a particularly beautiful one and swallow it whole. As you do this, be aware that you are taking within yourself the mystery of a creation shaped with love and given to the earth with love. Won Ton Communion, however, is more than cloud-swallowing. We can also take into ourselves a scarlet oak, a field ripe with grain, a lush green forest, a snow-carpeted valley or even a single glorious flower. How rarely do we take time to swallow, to take in and make part of ourselves, the rich feast of the Body of God! Busy, busy, we rush from event to event, giving creation only a quick glance. The Body of God, like any feast, requires time. If you decide to try it, you will find out that swallowing a whole cloud or a sunset takes time.

If our lives are to be Eucharistic, to be nourished by the gift of Christ, then the *soup de jour*, the soup of the day, must be Won Ton Sacred Soup. And if we are truly to go to Communion, to receive Christ's Body in its fullness, then that meal should begin with Won Ton Soup. For if we are not in communion with God's first great gift, the flesh and blood of God—creation— can we really be nourished by Christ, the second great gift? Like poor little Suppenkasper, we have neglected to eat our soup. Perhaps that is why we can dine upon the Body of Christ and still not become saints. Perhaps someone should place an empty soup bowl on **our** tombstones!

If we could include the *soup de jour* of a summer sunset as part of our daily ritual of prayer, the autumn appetizer of golden leaves, the silver soup of frost and snow and the bright-green tender-leaf soup of spring, then the religion which has not yet appeared, the religion that sings and celebrates the marriage of heaven and earth, **will** appear. Jesus, when speaking about the Kingdom, frequently used the image of a wedding feast. Each Mass, Lord's Supper or communion service is such a wedding feast. It celebrates that loving and intimate union between God and ourselves and between ourselves and creation. We are further called to celebrate this marriage of heaven and earth without any ''ifs'' or ''buts,'' without sometimes ''yes'' and sometimes ''no.'' From sex to serpents, we are invited to the great marriage feast in which all creation has become the Body of Christ, and so all creation is totally affirmed.

Because the true marriage of heaven and earth is so total, there are no reservations about it, and all we can say is, ''I love you with ALL my heart.'' For this reason, in the Catholic tradition, the Blessed Sacrament is reserved in all churches and chapels. A small part of the Supper of the Lord is kept in reservation in a tabernacle to proclaim that the love-union of Christ-with-us is no on-again off-again affair. It is a true marriage which proclaims constant fidelity. Christ is present not for a few moments at a certain celebration but continuously in both the outward sign and the deepest reality. The marriage, in short, IS.

The implications of this unfolding new religion of the marriage of heaven and earth has truly cosmic proportions. If we are truly to be the priestly people of this new covenant, we will have to acquire a wider, a cosmic, vision. Unfortunately, our holy communion tends not to be a whole communion. We need a universal vision of what is contained in the ritual act of Holy Communion, a vision that transcends any particular church affiliation. The time has come to move beyond the narrow confines of a Catholic Communion, Baptist Communion or Anglican Communion to a Christ Communion. In his letter to the Ephesians St. Paul wrote, "God has put all things under Christ's feet and has made him thus exalted, the head of the Church, which is his body: **the fullness of him who fills the universe in all its parts**" (Eph. 1: 22-23). If the fullness of Christ fills all the universe, then that must include not only the sun and the moon and distant galaxies but also clouds and caterpillars, wild-grasses and grapefruit.

Before we conclude this reflection, let's play around a little with that interesting word "if." What if, at the Last Supper, Jesus gave his disciples a gift that was beyond their wildest dreams, a gift whose implications they could not even begin to comprehend? What if that gift is also more than you and I even dare to imagine? What if—just, what if—at that Last Supper, Jesus took bread into his hands; giving thanks, he broke it and with hands outstretched toward those who sat around him, said, "This is my Body!" Then, turning, his hands still outstretched, he faced the open window looking out upon the turquoise twilight that touched the rolling hills around Jerusalem, upon the rooftops and winding narrow streets crowded with people and upon the giant, yellow full moon of spring rising over the Mount of Olives, and he said, "This is my Body!"

Seeing God in the Weather Report

Worship, prayer, reverence, love and service are part of the spectrum of fitting human responses to an awareness of the Divine Mystery. To be true such responses cannot be limited to one day a week or restricted to certain times in a single day. The response must be total, encompassing all times and places. While acknowledging that such a total response to God's love is logical, we also know it is far from easy. This is so partially because certain vital aspects of our daily life seem shut out from our prayers and worship. One such area is perhaps the most frequently discussed topic in our conversations and a fixture on every TV or radio news program. It also has a profound effect upon the economic, political, biological and even psychological dimensions of each of our lives. What is absent from our prayer responses to God? What is left out is the weather!

Perhaps you think I have overrated the importance of weather. But reflect first of all on how we use the weather as a greeting. "Nice day, isn't it?" Consider how we use it to begin a conversation. The daily weather is a natural, tension-relieving bridge for strangers or even friends to begin talking to one another. And "bad" weather has the magic to create an incredibly close bond among those who share it, even if they happen to be complete strangers. Without a doubt, too, the weather is important to all of us beyond our casual observation. A freeze in Florida skyrockets the cost of our morning orange juice. A prolonged drought in Russia or a serious flood in America's heartland can have international political consequences. The weather can even have a biological effect on us, causing colds, runny noses, sweating and sunburns.

Changes in the weather certainly cause changes in our emotions. Shifts in weather patterns alter the balance in groups of atoms in the atmosphere called ions. A growing school of scientists believe that different degrees of negative or positive ions influence a variety of emotions and feelings. Laboratory studies indicate that concentrations of negative or positive ions affect the levels of serotonin, a chemical which carries messages between the neurons of the brain. High winds and cloudy, dark days produce positive ions which can cause us to feel grumpy or worse. On the other hand warm, clear, sunny days produce negative ions, releasing more serotonin, and so we tend to feel cheerful, friendly and vigorous. Some people are more "weather-sensitive" than others, but we are all affected by changes in the elements.

So, if the weather has such a profound effect upon the whole of our lives, isn't it strange that it should be absent from our prayer and worship? That, however, was not always the case. In past ages the weather and worship were intimately united.

Examine the theologies—and the temples—of centuries past, and you will find a host of rain, wind, thunder, sun and moon gods. These weather gods of pre-Christian periods were among the most powerful of all ancient deities. Among the Phoenicians there was a mighty god named "Weather God." The Aztecs of Mexico worshiped Tlaloc, the rain god, an unyielding god to whom small infants were sacrificed. If the babies cried as they were being slaughtered by the temple priests, the people rejoiced because the tears were a sign of the rain that Tlaloc would shower upon their land. In every part of the world peoples worshiped gods and goddesses of the weather. The celebration of their feast days, at the changing of the seasons, the equinoxes and solstices, the cycles of the moon and other climatic events, was a natural expression of these peoples' awareness that religion must influence every aspect of life. It is paradoxical that pre-Christian religions, with their hundreds of gods who watched over everything from making love to making war, were so faithful to "praying always." One might ask why Christianity failed to incorporate such a vital part of human life as the weather into its worship.

Christianity is an evolved response to God, and a response that appeared only recently in human history. It had to address already existing nature religions which had such a sway over so many common people. As a result, Christianity never felt completely comfortable with nature. In a reaction against belief in the powerful nature gods, it closed its doors on creation and became an indoor religion. Today, even more deeply shaped by the industrialized, chrome-and-steel world of the West, Christianity seems ill-at-ease with the outdoors. The divorce between the weather and Christian religion in not total; some relics remain in our tradition. Among the psalms, for example, ice, sleet, hail, wind and sun are called upon to praise God. However, no official ceremonies or rituals of the Church are directly related to the weather or the changes in the seasons. Important feast days do occur around the solstices and equinoxes, but they are at best indirectly related to the weather or the seasons.

Contemporary Christians who pray the ageless psalms inside temperature-controlled chapels or churches (usually with stained-glass windows to block vision of the outside) tend to look upon ice and snow as inconveniences instead of cosmic prayers. The saying of one's evening prayers and the evening weather report seem worlds apart, but they need not be. Even Jesus was weather conscious. When asked by the Pharisees for some sign in the heavens, he replied, "When you see a cloud rising in the west, you say immediately that rain is coming, and so it does. When the wind blows from the south, you say it is going to be hot, and so it is. If you can interpret the portents of the earth and sky, why can you not interpret the present time?" (Lk. 12: 54-56).

Today we don't predict the weather by watching clouds rise in the west. We rather watch the evening news and the weather photo of our planet taken from a satellite more than 22,000 miles out in space! Indian rain dances, the sacrifices of infants to the god Tlaloc or prayers for rain seem totally inconsistent in an age of scientific wonder. Yet science need not separate us from God. It can rather draw us even closer to the real mystery of the Divine Mystery.

The weather is an important part of that Mystery. However, the questions remain, "How do we allow the weather to be part of our prayer?" and "Exactly how is the weather part of the mystery of God?"

Part of the answer can be found in understanding the unique nature of our universe which is not static but rather creatively unfolding. Scientific studies show how the act of creation did not cease billions of years ago but is still a divine dynamic process. Modern physics reveals to us a universe that is alive, full of spinning, expanding galaxies. These galaxies are expanding outward into space at enormous speeds. Some galaxies near ours are expanding at the rate of several thousand miles per second. Other far distant galaxies are expanding at a rate that approaches the speed of light. This means that we here on earth will never see their "star" light. Science also reveals to us that material things are not static or fixed as they appear but are composed of atoms united in a vast variety of dynamic patterns or structures. These atomic structures are in constant movement according to their temperatures and the thermal vibrations of their environments.

Earth also responds to its thermal vibrations. What we call weather is simply the effect of the sun's radiation upon our planet. Each day radiation equal to seventeen trillion kilowatts enters the earth's atmosphere from the sun. That heat causes warm air to rise from the regions near the equator. That warm air is then carried by the winds and meets cold air from the polar regions of our planet. This meeting, which effects the formation of high and low pressure pockets, creates the wonder we call weather. The weather, like other aspects of creation, is a mystery of movement and dynamic action. And that creation is an ongoing process in which the hands of the Divine Creator are still artistically at work. Whenever we are attuned to the atmospheric movement of the earth, attuned to its weather, we are also one with the Creator.

The weather, of course, is intimately connected with the seasons. So, when we are consciously in harmony with the seasons, the changes of the moon and the daily cycle of day and night, we are united with the cosmic worship of the universe. In the Vedic scriptures of India, the Divine Voice proclaims, "I am the Seasons." Prayer, then, can be a celebration of the Source of the Seasons in the midst of heat or rain, snow or wind, in the middle of winter or summer. But how could one celebrate such a liturgy of the seasons?

First, we can strive to enter fully into the flow of each day's weather. We can learn how to enjoy rainy days as well as sunny days, mindful that all weather is beautiful and sacred, as well as a part of the unfolding universe. The sacredness of the seasons was sung by Emily Dickinson in these verses:

> Oh, Sacrament of Summer days
> Oh, Last Communion in the Haze—
> Permit a child to join.

When you and I, like children, join in and make our communion with the summer heat or the winter chill, we participate in the sacrament of the seasons. Whenever we take time to be in communion with the weather, we discover that we are praying from a prayer book which holds a rich and timeless variety of prayers. Mark Twain once said of the weather in New England (which is likely to be true wherever you live), "I have counted one hundred and thirty-six different kinds of weather inside of twenty-four hours." That means one hundred and thirty-six different prayers for one day!

In addition, we can adapt our daily prayers to the seasons of the year. Usually our worship stands separate from the changes of weather and the changes of seasons—from the ebb and flow of the universe. As we said, we can make the snow or rain a part of our praise. We can also see in the seasons a mirror of our own emotional life. John Denver asked this musical question, "Do you see yourself reflected in the seasons?" In our moods and feelings we too have our winters and springs, our droughts and fertile times, our sunshine and showers.

Robert Frost wrote about this "heart weather" in his poem, "Tree at My Window":

> That day she put our heads together,
> Fate had her imagination about her,
> Your head so much concerned with outer,
> Mine with inner weather.

Frost's poetry can suggest images of the sudden rain showers of the heart that can be caused by an unkind word or a careless joke, as well as the unexpected sunshine of good news in the midst of a dreary day. Indeed we need to also listen carefully for each other's daily weather report if we are to live together in harmony and peace.

Another way to pray the prayer of weather is by celebrating the changing of the seasons. June 21, September 23, December 21 and March 21 are ancient magical feast days that announce the arrival of summer, autumn, winter and spring. These ageless feasts are filled with power when they are celebrated outdoors. Such times should remind us to look for every opportunity to pray out-of-doors. The universe is *the* Temple, and it is crowded with sacred shrines: lakes, forests, fields, streams, mountains and hills. Whenever we are outdoors and the weather embraces us with her abundant life, whether with steaming heat or a torrential downpour, let's not immediately run to some "weather-proof" place.

In the MGM movie *Singin' in the Rain*, Gene Kelly happily danced and sang in the midst of a downpour. Audiences delighted in his artistry and the magic of singing and dancing through a shower. But when you and I are "caught" in the rain, we usually neither sing nor dance but rather run for cover. Isn't it strange that only children beg, "Please, can't we go out and play in the rain?" Adults, who need ask no one's permission, rarely take advantage of opportunities for such "fun." They view rain only in practical aspects. To adults a rainy day means, "good for the garden" or "bad for the parade." However, a good rule of thumb for the transcendental is to remember that playgrounds of children make excellent prayer-grounds for adults.

Finally, since all good worship is both good art and good instruction, praying in communion with the weather can also be an excellent teacher for us. Usually we seek to control as much of life and as many people as we can. We dislike being "out-of-control" and so seek to "stay on top of things." The weather, however, is one thing we cannot control—or even predict with any accuracy. When we learn to play and pray with the weather—learn to flow with the ebbs and tides of unpredictable weather—we come to respect that both God and the elements are beyond control or manipulation. Such a blessed awareness makes us conscious of our creaturehood. It also makes us receptive to the unending flow of grace that comes from the divine heart. So instead of seeking to "control" the weather or the ways of God, we can live in holy communion with the seasons and with God. We can also "pray" our inner weather conditions and seasonal changes of the spirit by simply making them available to God just as they are. We can then watch ourselves and the universe unfold together in mysterious ways.

Take time today to "feel" the sun. As a Hindu mystic, Allama Prabhu, said, "Learn the taste of sunshine on the tongue." We can learn, without too much effort, to rejoice in the touch of the mist upon our faces, the south wind blowing through our hair or even the frost on our fingertips. Such spiritual exercises make us sensitive to those delicate, subtle gifts of nature that come to us each day, the gifts that we so often fail to notice. We can pause to be mindful, in gratitude, that these too are times of holy communion in the liturgy of the seasons, times when we can taste, feel and sense God. Surprisingly, we can also learn to rejoice in sudden, unexpected changes in the weather. Rejoice and open your being to the unique gifts of insight, awareness and joy that such changes can hold for you. James Riley expressed it this way:

> It hain't no use to grumble and complain,
> It's jest as easy to rejoice,
> When God sorts out the weather and sends rain,
> Why rain's my choice.

As you make the weather of this day "your choice," be mindful of the positive and negative ions that are invisibly dancing around you. Be aware too of the "inner weather" of your heart and of those who live with you. Seek sincerely to be in the flow of the universe as it expands outward into space. Remember, too, that in all these times you are in prayer. And if you can pray that prayer of the daily weather and the liturgy of the seasons, one with the continuous ebb-and-flow of the entire cosmos, then you will also be "in God." Your entire life will be richer and your holiness will be truly whole.

Bathtub *Beatitude*

Many of us retain a clear childhood memory of the traditional Saturday night bath in the family tub. One after another we took our turns in this family ritual. In many a family, the Saturday night bath was as important to proper attendance at church the next day as the ritual absolution from sin. Perhaps this primary home ritual of bathing was and is just that: ablution is absolution! Why do we submerge ourselves in water before a meeting with God? We are all familiar with the expression "Cleanliness is next to godliness," even if it is theologically incorrect. Purity, an inner condition of the heart, and not cleanliness, is actually next to godliness. But even a nodding acquaintance with religions indicates that both outward and inward cleanliness are essential for prayer.

In the Jewish tradition we find the *Mikveh* or ritual bath. This rite of bathing began as a purification for the priests who had come in touch with the blood of animals in the temple sacrifices. Contact with blood made a person unfit for worship, and so a ritual bath was necessary. In former times scribes also were obliged to take a ritual bath, a *Mikveh*, before they began to copy the Torah. This "holy" bath was to be taken in *Mayim Hayyim*, literally in living, flowing—not stagnant—waters. Today, this ancient custom has become a spiritual duty for the Hasidic Jews

who seek out the more mystical aspects of Judaism. Among the Hasidim it is customary to take this ritual bath on the eve of the Sabbath. Some even take it daily.

Hindus are also obliged to take a ritual bath in flowing waters. A text from the Vedic scriptures begins with the words, "O swiftly moving, purifying bath... ." For the traveler in India a common early morning sight is scores of people taking their sacred baths in the Ganges or another holy river.

Into this global tradition of "holy" bathing appeared John the Baptist, requiring that baths be taken in the flowing waters of the Jordan. John became the bath attendant for his cousin Jesus. In turn, a holy bath, Baptism, became the first sacrament and rite of initiation into his spiritual community, the Christian Church.

Hindu times of prayer, worship in the temple, attendance at the synagogue and initiation into the Community of Christ all involve a sacred bath. Is it possible that it is an action not only of cleansing but also of being immersed into God? Is a person immersed into a primal mystery as a prelude to being plunged into the Divine Mystery? If so, the Saturday night bath can hold greater power than we ever guessed as children. Its creative and recreative capacity is suggested right in the opening sentences of the Book of Genesis, "And the earth was a formless wasteland and darkness covered the abyss, while a mighty wind swept over the waters" (Gen. 1: 1). The creator, wind and water formed the primordial trinity.

Reflect for a brief moment on the fluid mystery of water. Nothing grows without its nourishment. From out of the waters of the oceans of this planet came life itself. Doesn't water remind us, even unconsciously, of our primal home? We all began life floating in the sea within our mothers' wombs. It should be no surprise, then, that most of us find water restful to watch or sit by and fun to play in. Water works wonderfully for us, but it also holds awesome destructive power. Floods and heavy rains can cause devastating damage and can even carry death. Although we are aware of this ravaging capacity, it is clear that water's benefits far outweigh its dangers. We regard water as one of our most faithful servants. "Go water and nourish the corn fields, satisfy the thirst of cattle, freeze yourself into cubes to chill our martinis, fill the sink and clean the dishes, fill the washer and clean our clothes, run generators to provide our electricity... ." Yet we often take water for granted and ignore the tremendous possibilities it holds for our holiness. All the while, Primal Mystery lurks right under our noses in the ice cube tray and in our bathtub.

Bathtubs today are not as popular as showers. The upright shower stall takes less room in construction and also uses less water. More importantly, bathing in a shower takes less time out of our busy lives. Taking a bath requires leisure. We need to fill the tub with water and allow time to soak and cleanse ourselves. Since most of us do not consider bathing a form of recreation or re-creation, and since we are all busy, we tend to get done with this "necessity" as rapidly as possible. In defense of bathing in a shower, it must be said that there is a certain sense of pleasure in its stinging briskness and massaging effect. It is also an excellent place to wash one's hair. But shower stalls lack the meditative and healing effects of a soak in a good hot bath. As the stress level increases in our hectic society, we may see a return to the slow soaking in a tub of hot water. The bathtub can become a place of refuge, cleansing and healing.

As you slip into your bathtub after a long, hard day, you may find that it is also a place of prayer. The steam, like the smoke of incense, rises slowly from the water. As it ascends, it can carry away all your aches and pains, all the burdens of the day. It can remove the residue of the day's frantic rushing still etched in your skin. When freed of distracting impediments, we are indeed much more ready, more responsive to meeting God face to face. All such preparations to make ourselves more receptive to the Divine Mystery are prayers in themselves!

Taking a shower or bath has become almost a daily duty. It is so common that it seems impossible for it to be prayer. Bathing and eating are so ordinary that we usually miss the Mystery inherent in both of them. Yet it is in these most common household activities that we touch the most ancient meeting places between

God and creation. Being immersed in water, whether bathing or swimming, awakens memories of humanity's womb, the ocean from which earth-life emerged. Something special happens to us when we are surrounded with the primal substance of water. Perhaps we unconsciously "remember" the urges of those long forgotten times. It is no coincidence that we feel so comfortable, so healed, so alive in water, since our bodies are over two-thirds water! Blood is 90% water and even muscles contain 80 to 90 percent. No wonder we are so much "at home" when we sit soaking in our bathtubs! It is really more a wonder that bathing has been overlooked as a prayer form in our incarnational Christian tradition.

Among Orthodox Jews there is a blessing recited before one takes a bath: "Blessed are you, Lord our God, King of the Universe, who has made us holy with your commandments and commanded us concerning immersion." Likewise in the Hindu religion there is a mantra, or chanted prayer, for taking a bath. The Vedas contain this beautiful prayer which we began earlier: "O swiftly moving, purifying bath, you flow gently down. With the help of the gods may my sins against mortals be washed away." We Christians have a tradition of praying before we eat, yet we lack a prayer or ritual expression before we bathe. Let's remember, however, that Christianity is still a young religion. There is room for "new" traditions, rituals and blessings to be born.

Each time we bathe or take a shower we could pray the Vedic prayer that our failings against God and one another might be washed away. We could chant a mantra as we slip into the hot, healing waters of a tub. Or we could, as is the custom of Catholics upon entering and leaving church, take a little water on our fingertips and make the sign of the cross. Usually such a sign is made only with holy water. But if we reflect on it, is not all water holy?

Why should we say a prayer or make a sign of the cross when we begin a shower or bath? Prayers before meals are not recited to bless the food since it has already been blessed by sun, rain and earth. It is rather to remind us that all food is holy, that it is a gift from God. If you are fully conscious of the gift of hot water in a tub or shower, in a world where only a small percentage of the population enjoys such a luxury, then you don't need to pray before enjoying it. If you are aware of the Divine Presence hidden in the primordial substance we call water, then no ritual sign is required. If you are wholly present to the water itself, to the memories of your prehistoric beginnings in it—if your mind is **full** of wetness, full of its healing touch—then, of course, there is no need to say any prayer, blessing or bathing mantra.

Whether or not this reflection stirs you to make yourself more conscious of the sacredness of bathing, I hope that it will encourage you to take more time in the tub or shower. Perhaps it will help you enjoy more the touch of water and all the pleasures of soaking in it. Especially for you who are over the age of forty, that may not be as easy as it first sounds. Pre-Vatican II Christian religious training surrounded any pleasures of the body, especially when it is naked, with extreme caution. To have sensual pleasure was to place oneself in grave danger of sin. Bathing, as a result, was reduced to a duty to be performed as quickly and inattentively as possible. But water, as well as the bathtub, is a gift from God who looked upon all that had been created as "good." We should always remember that the first and best way to show gratitude for any gift is to relish it.

The old-fashioned Saturday night bath held so many pleasures for us. As children it was a time to splash about and play with our rubber ducks and toy boats. On growing older it provided a time to think, reflect and be alone. Lost in that relaxing reflection, it was a time to forget about time—that is, until a knock came at the bathroom door and mother's voice brought back reality: "Edward, that's not your private tub! Your sister and brothers are all waiting for their turns. Hurry up now, and get dressed." Ah, these reflections and Saturday night baths both seem to go on longer than they should! So, aware that these thoughts on the prayerful pleasures and the pleasureful prayers of taking a bath have proceeded long enough, allow me to conclude with a quotation from Edmund Wilson's *A Piece of My Mind*:

> I have derived a good deal more benefit of the civilizing as well as the inspirational kind from the admirable

American bathroom than I have from the cathedrals of Europe...I have had a good many more uplifting thoughts, creative and expansive visions—while soaking in comfortable baths or drying myself after bracing showers...than I have ever had in any cathedral.

Life's Song

This book began with a story about a dog in hot pursuit of an elusive white rabbit. It is fitting that it conclude with a story about one that chased the Rabbit all the way Home.

Central to the Christian experience is the Resurrection. It speaks of Easter Sunday's joyous song sung in a sea of flowers. On the first Easter morning, however, the mood of Jesus' first disciples was strikingly different. As they gathered behind locked doors, if they sang at all, this could have been their song:

> Through all your life your greatest gift
>   was faithfulness that gave our spirits lift.
>   If love be true, it shone in you...
>   you were life's song.
> You were to all a pilgrim's friend;
>   you'd walk for miles their paths unto the end.
>   If love be true, it shone in you...
>   you were life's song.
> You gave much more than we returned;
>   you taught us more than we could ever learn.
>   If love be true, it shone in you...
>   you were life's song.
>
> On Easter dawn, alone you wished to be;

in quiet death you let your spirit free.
Once again we viewed mysteries through you;
you taught us well.
For if love be true, it shone in you...
you were life's song,
you were our joy,
in you was God.

Our faith in the Resurrection, if it is to be human as well as holy, must contain a balance of joy and sorrow. Such a faith is reflected in this song which speaks of the loss of someone who was to us "the song of life" and the incarnation of God.

To understand the fullness of the mystery of the Resurrection, we must be willing to peel back the veneer of Easter alleluias and see what is beneath them. We must be open to the tears and mourning of loss, the pain inherent in human love. Only when such emotions are allowed to sing their song can the expression of our faith be fully human and truly holy. Faith cannot be reduced to playing make-believe that the loss doesn't hurt. While the joy of the Resurrection is very real, we have not yet transcended the need to pass through the doorway of sorrow on the way.

St. John's vision of the future in the Book of Revelation images a beautiful city descending from heaven as a voice cries out, "This is God's dwelling, who shall wipe away every tear from their eyes; and there shall be no more death or mourning, or crying out in pain, for the former world has passed away" (Rev. 21: 3-4). However, as you and I await the fulfillment of that vision of the New Jerusalem, we live in **this** world. If our spirit quest and our faith are to be rooted in reality, then there must be room for the expression of both the divine and human within us.

Balance is the one art form that each of us must learn, for humanity has the habit of swinging from one extreme to the other in a relatively short time. Not very long ago, funerals and burials of Christians were black, mournful, gloomy occasions. The burden of human failings, impending judgment for past sins and the need for redemption sang out louder than our belief that the deceased person was to share in the promise of the resurrection and victory of Christ. Today we have seemingly swung a full 180 degrees in the opposite direction. Contemporary funerals are all white, brimming over with Easter joy, echoing alleluias. Weeping and mourning are viewed as almost heretical, as a denial of faith. Hard to find in our funerals are rituals and songs that express mourning and grief at the loss of those we have loved.

If the one we have lost in death was for us our "life's song," then that loss is truly a terrible blow. Indeed, we believe that the loved one, the "song" that fueled our existence, is now incorporated into the Divine Mystery, but we will not feel the touch of or see our loved one again. That realization is perhaps the greatest pain known to the human heart. The death of our "life's song" is truly the heart attack we fear most.

Because of that fear many never risk loving another with all their hearts. We all know that the greater the love, the more pain of loss that must be endured. So, many cut back, loving with only half a heart to reduce that pain when the time comes. Such fear is human and normal, but it is also a denial of our belief that there is a resurrection, that there is life beyond this life. Fundamentally, it is a denial that love is stronger than death. Real faith in the Resurrection implies learning how to love fully.

Yet, again, even if our faith is great enough to move the Rocky Mountains into the Gulf of Mexico, it is an undeniable part of the human condition to experience profound loss. The agony that makes weeping and mourning the spontaneous outpouring of our hearts is intimately linked to our having loved dearly. Our Christian belief in life and love beyond the grave must never leave out the human *and* the animal—yes, the **animal**—for our belief is in the resurrection of the body as part of the Mystical Body of Christ.

The song that began this reflection was not written about Christ or the apostles. It is the work of Tom Turkle of the Forest of Peace community in which I live, and it was written at the death of our beloved dog Shiloh! Part German Shepherd and part Doberman, for eleven years he was an essential part of our life and community. Shiloh was the companion for countless guests who walked the paths of the forest. He was our gentle guru who taught us much about being natural. On Easter Sunday several years back, we found him sleeping peacefully in death beside a small stream, just across our fence-line in our neighbor's field. While the song (I'm sorry that you only have the words) was about our dog, it is also about Christ! We believe that this song expresses the mystery of Christ that we experienced in our dog Shiloh. Christ in a dog? That sounds like madness!

Recall, however, those haunting words of St. Paul to the early Christian community at Ephesus: "God has put all things under Christ's feet and made him thus exalted, the head of the Church, which is his body, the fullness of him who fills the universe in all its parts" (Eph. 1: 22-23). Look again at those last words and reflect on them: "...who fills the universe in all its parts."

We know that in our galaxy alone there are over one-hundred billion suns, splendrous stars of enormous size. And in the whole universe there are over one-hundred billion galaxies spanning distances that are beyond the comprehension of our small minds. At night as you stand outside and look up at the night sky, ponder the mystery that the "fullness" of Christ is now present in all the billions of stars and galaxies that fill the universe. Be aware too of how that same Sacred Mystery also fills your dog who sits faithfully beside you!

Each year at the first full moon of spring we celebrate the feast of Easter, which proclaims that the Head of the Body has already risen from the tomb and has expanded outward to fill the universe. We celebrate as well the fact that we, the Body, are soon to follow. Paul of Tarsus was the first Christian writer to reveal how God intended all creation to share in that spiritual transformation of the Resurrection. In another letter, Paul wrote to the community at Rome, continuing his theology of the Easter event:

> I consider the sufferings of the present to be as nothing
> compared to the glory to be revealed in us. Indeed, the
> *whole* of the created world eagerly awaits the revela-
> tion of the children of God...yet not without hope,
> because the world itself will be freed of corruption and
> share in the glorious freedom of the children of God.

> Yes, we know that all creation groans and is in agony
> even until now (Rom. 8: 18-22).

To look forward, then, to the resurrection of our beloved Shiloh is not as heretical as it may have first sounded. And if God was truly speaking through Paul of Tarsus, perhaps we should take a second look at heaven and at who the citizens of the New Jerusalem will be. Angels and saints will be there, yes, but also crocodiles, parakeets and birds of ten thousand different plumages, elephants and possum, horses and cows, cats and dogs, and even ants and cockroaches! Such a heaven is only the logical—if not theological—conclusion to our belief that God never breaks a promise.

As old Noah came out of his rain-soaked ark, God promised, "See, I am now establishing my covenant with you and your descendants after you and with every living creature that was with you; all the birds and various tame and wild animals that were with you and came out of the ark...This is the sign that I am giving for all ages to come, of the covenant between me and you and every living creature...on earth" (Gen. 9: 9-12, 17).

We believe as part of our creed that God never breaks a promise or covenant. So we can assume that those who have entered heaven ahead of us must have had quite a shock! The pearly gates swung open not so much to a New Jerusalem, a heavenly city, but to a New Eden—or a New Ark floating serenely on a sea of galaxies.

We rejoice that the love we shared with Shiloh has eternal consequences. We believe that on that Easter Sunday Shiloh knew intuitively that death's bright angel was coming, and he went to meet it. Shiloh never left our property except to accompany a guest for a walk on the road. But on that morning he began the most awesome journey that any of us can take—going forth to meet death. A few feet into our neighbor's field, the New Jerusalem, robed in splendor like a bride, swooped down out of the sky to meet him. The great mystery that our budding primitive minds cannot yet even begin to fathom swept up our beloved Shiloh and incorporated him into the fullness of that which we call God.

The purpose of these Rabbit Reflections is to encourage and nourish your spiritual life. But what is your spirituality if not the lifestyle that flows from what you believe. Spirituality is more than the sum of our prayers, spiritual disciplines, times of solitude and meditation: it is the full expression of how we live. It includes how we treat the earth, our food and the family cat, how we love others and our possessions. While we profess a communal creed at times of worship, our personal creeds, even though they are usually unconscious and never prayed aloud, are very real too. Now, if one's personal creed includes a statement such as, "I believe that the fullness of Christ fills the universe in all its parts...that God keeps all covenants and pledges," then the implications are both beautiful and awesome.

The rainbow, God's covenant sign to Noah and the rest of creation, is a springtime sacrament. Its appearance in the sky never fails to invoke joyful surprise and appreciation. But one has to wonder if our pets, as well as birds and cattle and other creatures, may look up at a rainbow and see in it something that we humans miss.

This reflection on the full implications of the resurrection of the body is intended to give you a new way of looking at your relationship with the creatures with whom you share life, even if you don't have a personal pet. May each rainbow you behold be something more than a natural phenomenon. May it be a sign of the fullness of God's plan for creation—the resurrection of all the dead.

I have one more thought in closing. I don't know about you, but I have never had any special wish about what happens at my funeral, as long as it's kept simple. But recently a strong desire has surfaced. I wouldn't feel comfortable making a funeral request, however, unless I felt that it would help me be more zealous in my attempts to be who I would like to be.

It's all too easy to take the least difficult path, especially as one grows older. Age does have its privileges, and one of them is the built-in excuse: "I'm too old." It's often used to justify half-hearted loving, a lack of creativity, irritation over little things and a slackening of zest for life. But the new desire for my funeral helps me to not fall into that trap. My motto for the coming years: "NO EXCUSES!"

And the funeral request? I would like to have the song written for our dog Shiloh sung at my funeral. Look again at the words; read them slowly. Perhaps you might also find in that song something about who you would like to be and how you would like to be remembered:

> If love be true, it shone in you...
> you were our song,
> you were our joy,
> in you was God.

WHEN
YOU LIVE
ON A SMALL
PLANET YOU SOON
REALIZE THAT WHAT
YOU PURSUE IS
ALSO PURSUING
YOU.

ACKNOWLEDGEMENTS

The writing and publishing of any book is a team sport, requiring the same talented interplay of gifts as a championship basketball team.

I gratefully acknowledge my teammates, without whose gifts this book would never have come into your hands.

> **Thomas Skorupa**, for his creative editing of the manuscript.
> **Thomas Turkle**, for his skill as managing editor and publisher.
> **Paula Duke**, for her proofreading and assistance in editing—along with the rest of the Shantivanam community with whom I live.
> **Steve Hall**, for his assistance as the printer—along with the rest of the fine staff at Hall Directory.